From Chicago Bus Driver to The God Man

Charles M. Christensen Life Stories

RAE ANN FUGATE

WESTBOW®
PRESS
A DIVISION OF THOMAS NELSON
& ZONDERVAN

Scripture taken from the King James Version of the Bible.

WestBow Press books may be ordered through booksellers or by contacting:

WestBow Press
A Division of Thomas Nelson & Zondervan
1663 Liberty Drive
Bloomington, IN 47403
www.westbowpress.com
1 (866) 928-1240

Because of the dynamic nature of the Internet, any web addresses or links contained in this book may have changed since publication and may no longer be valid. The views expressed in this work are solely those of the author and do not necessarily reflect the views of the publisher, and the publisher hereby disclaims any responsibility for them.

Any people depicted in stock imagery provided by Thinkstock are models, and such images are being used for illustrative purposes only.
Certain stock imagery © Thinkstock.

ISBN: 978-1-4908-3981-3 (sc)
ISBN: 978-1-4908-3982-0 (hc)
ISBN: 978-1-4908-3983-7 (e)

Library of Congress Control Number: 2014910271

Printed in the United States of America.

WestBow Press rev. date: 06/20/2014

CONTENTS

Dedication vii

Preface ix

John Kruk and His Strength 1

Birth - Early Years 3

Teen Years... 9

Young Married Years 18

Starting a Family and as a Streetcar Conductor 27

From Streetcar Conductor to Bus Driver 31

The One Terrible Accident 36

My Life Changed In A Second 39

Beginning Effects of Life Changes 50

Christine 56

The Move to Wonder Lake and Retirement 59

Church Responsibilities and Family Blessings 64

More Streetcar Stories from 1936 to 1946.................. 73

Bus Driving Experiences 82

The Blind Bus Driver 97

Another Story Never Published 104

Nothing Ever Happens... 105

A Young Woman Who Needed Help........................... 114

James.. 117

The College Man and The Philosophy of Life.............. 122

Other Ministries..................................... 124

Working With Our Pastor 128

Bob the Hitchhiker................................ 133

Peterson The Cheat and a Run-In with a Supervisor ... 136

The Horrible Blizzard of 1967 144

1991 In Retirement................................147

Was There a Serial Killer on my Bus?........................ 150

Pay the Fare or Pay the Consequences 152

The Bartender's Kindness 155

The Man Who Could Not Sleep.................. 158

The Man Who Tried My Patience.............. 162

Current Days 167

The Last Story 169

Afterword... 173

DEDICATION

This book is dedicated to Clem and Marie Bilhorn and to Charles R. Bartels and to everyone who was involved with the ministries of the Mayfair Bible Church in Chicago in the early 1950s. Without their dedication to the Lord and their faithfulness in prayer for our family the following story may not have been possible. They have our family's profound gratitude and we praise the Lord for them and for His faithfulness to all of us.

PREFACE

My Dad, Charlie (Bus) Christensen, gave me cassette tapes that he recorded periodically over the years. They contain stories of his life as a husband, father, Chicago Surface Lines streetcar conductor and Chicago Transit Authority bus driver. They are not necessarily in chronological order but are told as they came to his mind over the years of dictating. I have rewritten them for clarity and readability. You will read about how God changed him in mid-life from an ordinary man into a man of God.

In some instances I changed the name of someone for privacy reasons.

Photographs are from the files of The Chicago Transit Authority and are used with permission.

Rae Ann Fugate

To my new friend Mike,

May God bless you richly

Rae Ann Fugate

JOHN KRUK AND HIS STRENGTH

There was an old Austrian named John Kruk, a guttural speaking man who was physically strong and a giant. We worked together on the streetcars in Chicago. He was much older than I was. He had been a sergeant in the Austrian army and stories were told about him around the streetcar barn. When he first came over to the United States he drove a beer wagon drawn by four horses, delivering barrels of beer. A barrel of beer weighs four hundred pounds. One time he went into a saloon where he was delivering a keg of beer and said to the bartender, "Where you want?" John was limited in his English speech. "Where you want?" He meant the four hundred pound barrel of beer.

The bartender contemptuously said, "Oh, put it up on the bar." John Kruk took the four hundred pound barrel of beer and set it up on the bar. "Oh, no!" the bartender said, "I didn't really mean that. Don't put it up there." He came around the end of the bar excitedly gesturing for John to take the barrel down.

John said, "You said put on bar. I put on bar. You take it down," and he left. That incident shows John's strength but there was another incident I actually witnessed. We had a late run on the streetcar one night. We were working one of those split runs where we operated the streetcar for a few hours in the morning and then we came back in the late afternoon to work the rush hours until about nine o'clock at night. This was on Western Avenue. John and I had left Howard Street and were coming down Western Avenue to Division Street to pull into the barn. When we got down to Division Street, I was supposed to run off the back end of the streetcar, run up to the front of the car, and lift the switch which allowed John to drive the streetcar around off of Western Avenue onto Division Street.

There was a man, probably in his twenties, sitting in the front seat of the streetcar and he was drunk. I had gotten everybody off, but this man did not pay any attention when I said, "Far as we go." I went in and shook him but I could not wake him up. He was perfectly sound asleep. There was no way I could get him up and off the car. I shook him and hollered, "You have to get off here." There was no response.

John opened the sliding door between his driving platform and the passenger cabin and said, "What you wait for?"

"Oh," I said, "John, this man is sleeping, he's drunk, and I can't wake him up."

He said, "I wake." He walked up to the man, grabbed him just below the lapels of his suit coat, and lifted him out of the seat. The man must have weighed 170 or 180 pounds. John literally shook him awake. He said, "You wake up now. You get off and go home. Come" and he half dragged the man off the streetcar. I made sure the guy got over onto the sidewalk before I lifted that switch. But that was John Kruk. I became quite fond of him and remember him often.

BIRTH - EARLY YEARS

I think I am getting ahead of myself here. Maybe I should start with my growing up years and how I became a bus driver in Chicago.

At the beginning of my life on February 29, 1912 my mother and dad owned a rooming house at 2100 West Warren Boulevard. My sister, who was two-and-a-half years older than me, was born in this home. I was born in the hospital.

In later years I always reminded people that many great men, such as President Abraham Lincoln, President George Washington and many others, were born in February including myself, Charles Martin Christensen. Not that I was bragging or anything like that. It was not until many years later that I realized for me to be born in February it had to be a leap year when there was an extra day. Otherwise I would have been born in March. Also, I was born after 11:00 p.m. so I barely got in under the February deadline.

My sister's name was Ellen Margaret Christensen. Margaret was the name of a lady who roomed with my mother and dad and became a life-long friend of the family. Margaret called my sister Girly. That was her nickname. Margaret, bless her heart, named me Buster because I had a Buster Brown hair cut in my first two years.

I was two years old when Ellen died. I do not have any personal remembrance of her but we have a lovely picture of her, at the age of four-and-a-half, in a gold frame that hangs in my home, and every once in a while I have a little word with the picture, knowing Girly is with God and I will see her in the near future. Girly died of diphtheria. I guess they did not have shots in those days. She got sick and died within four days and I can assume that was an extremely difficult time for my parents.

I do not know how long my parents kept that house but it must have been six or seven years, at least, because one of the few things I remember in that early childhood is when my mother took one of those child's wagons and pulled it down to the coal yard, with Raymond in her arms, to beg or buy, two bags of coal to heat the house. I think that must have been around 1918 during the war when coal was hard to get. I do not know for sure about those facts. I do not know how old I was when we later moved to Belden Avenue and Springfield Avenue in Chicago.

One other thing that occurred during my preschool years was a snowstorm where the snow was piled up so high that when I looked out the living room window toward the street, all I could see go by was the top of a milk wagon. In those days it was horses and wagons more than automobiles and trucks. I could not see the horse or the man driving. That remains in my memory from that time.

I had a brother named Raymond who was born two-and-a-half years after me. Raymond and I, as far as I am concerned, had a good boyhood, and we got along fairly well although we were of quite different natures. He was an athletic fellow. I was average at athletics. I did not make any teams within the school system. We went our separate ways almost from boyhood. There was a dissimilar thinking within our hearts and minds and although we got along well there was no closeness as brothers. However, I loved him.

When Mom and Dad moved over to Belden Avenue and Springfield Avenue my dad got a job as a streetcar conductor on the Chicago Surface Lines and worked there for six years. I began school on Belden Avenue. I remember that I had a disability. I lisped. I could not say the letter S and had to take a little special training when I started school to help me overcome this obstacle. Once I did, I was able to go through school without any difficulty.

In Chicago, when you went from first to eighth grade, you went from 1B as the first semester to 1A as the second semester and then to the next grade from 2B to 2A and so on. My years there were uneventful and I passed my tests. I must have done fairly well, because when I was in 7A and was to be promoted to 8B, I went right into 8A. I do not know that I was that intelligent but I did skip a semester. I graduated at the age of thirteen from the Mozart Grammar School.

I remember an incident when I was in sixth or seventh grade. I was on my way home from school and some of the boys who were in the workshop (I was not in the workshop) were also on their way home. They had little square boxes with a wire attached to the top. This little wire hung down but when the boys took the end of it and scratched it on a piece of metal also attached to the tops of the boxes noise came out of them. They called them radios. These were our very first radios and my schoolmates had made them in school. Remember, there was no such thing, in my day, as radio or television.

We did have a wind-up Gramophone and records at our home. The records were a quarter inch thick and cut on only one side. They were 78 rpms (revolutions per minute), and the voices on them were Gallagher and Enrico Caruso, and other famous opera singers. The music was beautiful. I inherited some of those records from my aunt Georgia. When she died we cleaned out the place where she lived and I found a half dozen or so of them. I kept them for a few years and then gave them to Bruce Damschroder, my son-in-law, Deanne's husband, because he seemed to be interested in old radios and things like that. I do not know what became of them.

Well, here I was now on Belden Avenue. I must have been around six or seven when we moved to the Belden Avenue and Springfield Avenue area. I met several boys in the neighborhood and we played games. We had roller skates with steel wheels. Of course, we played all the games on roller skates. The rules were that we could not go past the curb on either side of the street. We could not go by the next street south of us or north of Belden. We had to stay on the street to play the games and we played a lot of types of games.

One other thing, my mother and dad apparently trusted me. They bought me a Daisy Air Rifle that held one hundred shots in it. We lived in a basement flat that was two cement steps down from the laundry room. It was a four or five room flat in the basement. Whenever we got a gully washer of heavy rain the water would come up through the floors and flood our little flat with two to three inches of water. After it quit raining Dad and Mom had to flush out the whole flat and clean up everything and start all over again. My Dad was janitor of this flat building as well as working as a conductor on the streetcars. Well, as I say, I had this BB gun.

Now outside our front door were steps up into the laundry room. The laundry room was, roughly, thirty feet long. On the other side of it was a doorway into the boiler room. At the other side of the boiler room there was a coal bin which was partitioned off with heavy boards. The partition blocked the coal from spilling out all over the place. On the other side of the partition there was an opening in the outside wall, like a small door. The coal company delivered coal as ordered, dumping it from the back of a dump truck into the bin. Then Dad shoveled it into the fire. We had a Herbert Downdraft Boiler and he fed it Pocahontas Mine Run coal.

When I had this Daisy Air Rifle, I used to have little ten pins, about one-and-a-half to two inches tall, I do not remember exactly, and I used to put a stepladder way back by that wooden partition in the coal bin and set these ten pins up on every area of the ladder. I would go back the thirty feet down those two cement steps into our little flat and I would sit there and shoot those "bad guys" off of the ladder. Man, I won the war every time. And I had a good time. I was a good shot. I must have spent hours doing that in my youth because when we moved, there were thousands of BB holes in that partition behind the stepladder. It was just loaded with lead BB marks where the BBs had struck it. I had a really fantastic time doing that.

Mother gave my brother and me ten cents on Sunday mornings and sent us about a mile west on Belden Avenue to the Baptist Sunday school. Now I was a very good boy. I used to give a nickel of my dime in the offering plate and spent just a nickel on myself. Would you say that is fifty per cent of my income rather than tithing, which is ten percent?

I had a good conscience about this. I do not know what Ray ever did with his dime.

Raymond and I went to vacation Bible school at that church, and when I was twelve years old, I made a hammock by knitting or macramé or whatever they called it. As I worked on the hammock, one of the teachers came to me and began talking to me concerning my relationship with Jesus Christ. He asked if I was saved or not. I do not remember who it was or any details. All I know is that I was embarrassed and I did not go back to Sunday school after that. I never even went to church until after I was thirty-nine years old. The story of that will come later.

As I said, Dad worked as a streetcar conductor on the Chicago Surface Lines on Fullerton Avenue, just a block north of us. It ran east and west. There were times when I went out and rode with him while he was working on that street. The only problem was, after going back and forth two or three times I got car sick and hung out one of the windows throwing up. Oh, I was quite a guy! Dad worked there for six years and then he joined the janitors' union and took another job and we moved again.

This time we moved to 2410 North Kilbourn Avenue right on the corner of Fullerton Avenue and Kilbourn Avenue. Kilbourn Avenue was 4500 west in Chicago. Fullerton was 2400 north. Dad took care of a 36-apartment building that stood on that corner plus two 8-flats north of it, one across the alley and one across the corner. So he had a total of fifty-two apartments in three buildings and he was the janitor of all them. Now-a-days we would call him a maintenance engineer.

TEEN YEARS

At age thirteen I began attending Carl Schurz High School as a freshman and spent my four years there. I do not recall a great deal about the early years. I guess I did what I had to do through my senior year. The only problem was that I was more interested in sports than I was in school. At the beginning of my 4B class I had become friends with Eddie Sherman and we ran around together quite a bit. In fact, we ran around so much that I neglected my homework. I had four solids: I had history, science, geography, and mathematics, and I took typing as a special extra curriculum.

Because I was too busy to turn in my homework, in the first quarter of that 4B class, I wound up with three failing red marks on my report card, in history, science, and geography. I did get by in math. I was pretty good at arithmetic and the early mathematics that I had to learn. I did not think anything of those red marks. I brought my report card home for my Mom's signature but she did not say too much. In the second and third quarters, I had three red marks in the same subjects. At the end of the third quarter my report card showed a nice little solid square of nine red marks and I was failing in three of the subjects. My mother still did not chastise me. She must have been a wise woman. What she did way was, "Bus, if you do not graduate with your class you will not graduate." That was all she said. But for some reason, beyond my comprehension, it scared the life out of me. I wanted to graduate with my class. Boy, if I did not graduate with my class, what would I do? During the fourth quarter I studied everything I was supposed to. I got an average of 85 across the board on all my lessons and I did all of my homework. I passed all the tests. I was capable of doing the work; it was just that I was lazy. I passed in three of those subjects, geography, science and English but my history teacher, Miss Hallushka failed me in history.

I knew I had to do something about that so I went down to the school office and got permission to take 4B history and 4A history in the 4A class of my senior year. I had finally figured out the importance of doing my work. In 4A I passed all subjects all the way through and graduated in June, 1929. I did not receive any special honors. I always say I passed by the skin of my teeth but I do appreciate the fact that I did get by.

During those teen years I began working with my dad on those apartment buildings. He was the custodian, and my job was to empty the garbage every day. There were six three-story stairwells in that big building and four two-story stairwells in the two 8-apartment buildings. I had to empty all the garbage. In the big building we had a garbage burner in addition to the regular boiler.

I should mention, for those interested in these things, that the big building had a Herbert Downdraft boiler. Dad would build a fire in the pit and as the fire burned, the coals would fall down onto coils of water pipes. As the coils heated up, the water in them built up steam pressure. The steam would rise up into the pipes of the radiators in the apartments to heat them up. Within two hours it would burn itself through in one particular spot and the fire would fall down into that hole in this downdraft and if Dad did not get to the basement to break up the fire and remake it he would lose the steam pressure. He needed to keep the pressure in the building at three to four pounds on a constant basis although at night he let it go down a little bit.

In the Herbert Downdraft, in the winter time, we burned one ton of coal a day to heat that big building. That was a lot of coal and a lot of shoveling. Many years later, just before my Dad left there, the building owner installed a screw type feeder that had a bin on it. Dad would fill up the copper bin and the coal would be fed through to the fire pot with a huge screw that went out into the fire pot. It was not really as efficient as Dad's work because it did not smooth the fire out as much as he did. My job was to take care of that.

Now the other two buildings had Kewanee boilers which were fantastic. I would go and throw a few shovels of coal in those boilers, and they held the steam for hours. They were extremely favorable boilers as far as we were concerned.

Another of my jobs was to flush down the stairwells in the big building with a water hose once a week. Raymond got a job with the milk wagon driver helping him deliver bottles of milk to people's homes. He did not do any of the work around those buildings. This was my job and it was satisfactory. There were no arguments or fighting between us, we each took the job that we wanted. Ray got paid by the milk man. I do not know what he earned but not much, I'm sure, in those days.

Another way I earned money was to collect all of the discarded newspapers that the tenants tossed out. I collected them in all of these buildings. Now, mind you, I got sixty-five cents per one hundred pounds of newspaper in those days, and I collected at least a thousand pounds of newspaper every month. There was a Jewish man, a rag picker, who came every month to pick up all the newspapers I had saved. I had them stacked and tied and I also saved any metal I found. I sold the paper and the metal to my rag picker friend and that would be my money, my pay, for working around the building.

Also, during those hard times, I had some business cards printed up. I had a friend named Russell. We were not together very long, but we had some cards printed up, *Bus and Russ Window Washers, fifteen cents per window.* Russ never did enter into this project but I did. There were eleven windows in each flat in that big building. I had regular customers, some on the third floor, and I went up and sat on their windowsills and washed those windows inside and out. It took forty-five minutes to an hour to clean eleven windows. I used a chamois and cloth and just wiped them all clean, and I did good work. My customers complimented me on my work. I earned $1.65 for those eleven windows. I was a very nice boy, a fine fellow, however, a cynic.

In my high school days I met a young man named Christian Christensen, the same last name as mine. There was no family connection between us. His dad owned and operated a tavern. Every Sunday morning, at his father's house, we played penny ante poker. Chris and I played there every Sunday morning. Sometimes his father joined us. Otherwise there were other teens in the neighborhood, who played, or other people, maybe six or eight of us down there playing poker. I really enjoyed that.

Chris and I, often times, went down to the pool hall down at Fullerton Avenue and Pulaski Road, about a mile east of us, and played a game called Kelly Pool. Now on a pool table there are fifteen balls, numbered 1 to 15. There was also a little shaker with fifteen little round disks in it, called pills or peas, numbered 1 through 15. Each player would shake up the shaker and roll out one pill which he kept secret from the other players. Everyone who played in the game took one of these pills with the number of a ball on it. This was his ball in this game. Now if a player knocked one of the other guy's numbered balls into the pocket, on his turn of playing, he would get a nickel from him. If a player knocked his own ball into the pocket, he got a dime from every one of the other players. Chris and I were both pretty good pool players, and we played two to three hours, and made enough money to pay our share of the pool game and have ourselves a couple of dollars. Then we went across the street to the bookie and played the horses. We would bet fifty cents on a horse to win or place, and if we won five, six, or ten dollars that evening we could go to the show, or out to eat. We had a good time.

I mention this because it is vitally important at this point. There was no religion at this time in my life. I was a good teen-ager, obedient to my parents and I did not like to drink. I did smoke cigarettes at seventeen. I was not into drugs and I was a virgin. I was very shy, believe me or not, those of you who know me, you may not believe this, but I was a very shy young man.

There were some good points in the pool hall. I remember one time when Coca Cola brought out a great advertisement. They were bringing The Masked Marvel to the pool hall and he was going to demonstrate tricks on the pool table. Chris and I went to the hall and I thought, oh boy! This is going to be fun. You got all the Coca Cola you could drink and that was in the days when it was in those funny shaped little bottles. Maybe some of you younger people do not remember that, but they had these small bottles of Coke, maybe six or eight ounces in a bottle. I could drink all I wanted at this show. I thought that was fantastic. I had a hard time getting through my second bottle of Coca Cola, however, as the man demonstrated trick shots on the pool table that were fantastic. I never forgot that. In fact, just a few years ago at the resort area where we go to camp with our little trailer, a man came and showed us some of his tricks on the pool table. It was really great. I tried a few of them myself but it takes a lot of practice and a good pool player to accomplish many of them. It takes know-how in operating a pool stick and the balls.

I had another friend named William. He was a lady's man at seventeen. His dad had been a saloon owner and when he died he left his wife $100,000 in life insurance so they had money. Willy bought a new car every year or two, and we went driving around. Whenever Willy saw girls we knew along the way he wanted to stop but I always seemed to have homework to do and I went home.

I was taught a lesson by Willy. He came to me one day and said he and another fellow were going downtown to State and Lake Streets to have some fun. They were going to flirt with the street girls. I begged off again. I did not like the idea. I was too shy for that type of thing. They went downtown that night. The next day, Will came to me and said, "Bus, you've got to go with me."

I said, "Where, Will."

He said, "I've got to go down to Grand Avenue and State Street. There's a doctor down there."

I said, "Why do you have to see the doctor?"

"I got to go down and get a shot against gonorrhea or syphilis, or whatever," he said. He told me he had fooled around and had sex with a woman in a hallway downtown the night before. He was scared stiff that he might have picked up a disease. So I went with Will to this doctor's office. He drove and when we got there I went up to the doctor's office with him. The doctor gave him a shot and we went back home. He had to wait ten days before he could be sure he had not caught anything. Will sweated those ten days out and I will tell you, it taught me a life time lesson, that illicit sex is not important. It is not satisfying. It brings nothing but harm and trouble in the long run. So, I am glad of that.

As I said, neither Chris nor I were drinkers, however, his dad did make homemade wine. One Halloween Chris, his older brother, Wally, and I got hold of their dad's wine and they began drinking. I had a glass, I guess, but that was enough for me. I did not like it. It did not sit too well with me, and that was all I wanted. After we drank we went to the Embassy Theater. That was also on the corner of Pulaski and Fullerton. While we were in the theater poor Chris got so drunk he could not stand up and he threw up all over the lobby. Wally and I had to carry him out to the car and Wally had to drive him home and put him to bed. That was another lesson I learned, that it did not pay to allow liquor to take over your body.

I mentioned I was shy. I did have a girlfriend, that is, a girl that I dated. I called her up and asked to take her out to the theater. I think her name was Bethel. The thing that fascinated me about this girl, who was about sixteen, is that she was such a fantastic piano player that she taught other pupils. She had about six students and this fascinated me. I thought Bethel was a fine girl. I called her up on Wednesday and went to her house to pick her up on Saturday and then we went to the theater. This was a routine date for us. We walked to and from the theater hand in hand and sometimes we looked in the furniture store windows and talked about furnishing a place. I was quite taken with this girl. I was nearly seventeen.

I called her up one Wednesday. She said, "Charles, I'm going to go steady with Ronald and so I won't be seeing you anymore." Now here was a fellow with a broken heart. I must have just turned seventeen. My friend Russell came over and I cried to him about this. We went out to the delicatessen and bought ten cents worth of summer sausage and one of those large dill pickles. Then we went down in the basement where I lived and we sat and cried together, not really cried, but we moaned and groaned about the loss of this girlfriend.

I must have gotten over it pretty quickly because that same year, in the fall of my seventeenth year, just before my eighteenth birthday, we went to a dance at one of the schools.

I was not a good dancer but I liked the music and I liked the companionship and so I went along to the dance. That is where I saw Grace Minerva Poole, this lovely girl. And it was love at first sight, I am sure; it had to be love at first sight. I asked her for a dance and we danced. At that time there were several young Filipino lads in the area, sophisticated, excellent dancers, and how shall I say it? They were open and broad minded and I thought they were bad-mannered.

While I was dancing with Grace she said, "One of the Filipino fellows wants to dance with me all the time and I don't like dancing with him." So, when I saw him dancing with her I would go up and tap him on the shoulder to cut in. I would dance away with Grace and she thanked me for that. She did not like his manners, either.

I do not know how our relationship progressed because we usually went out as a group. I tried to be near Grace all of the time. There was, however, another young man named Henry who was seeking her favor. She had been dating Henry before she met me. I was jealous. Me, Charles, jealous? Of course not! Well, anyway, we went out as a group to different places.

One time we were playing tennis at the court in our neighborhood and Grace and I were partners. I was at the net and she was in the background when a ball came over the net, and I went for it, and missed it. She walked up behind me and swatted me on the seat with her tennis racket. She said, "What's the matter with you? How come you missed that one?" and I turned around and took hold of her and hugged her to me and kissed her hard, right on the lips. Boy. What a bold fellow! I even amazed myself. I was truly; I don't know what, maybe astounded that I would do such a thing.

YOUNG MARRIED YEARS

Grace and I went together for two solid years. I was eighteen; she was sixteen when we began dating. We held hands, walked in the parks, went out somewhere in the evening, came home and sat in her front hall and talked as long as we dared, whispering because we did not want her mother and dad to hear us. I loved this girl. Of course, I never laid a finger on her. She was a virgin and so was I. I loved her, and so I honored her. However, a couple doesn't go together for two years without having feelings come to the fore. I remember standing up one night, ready to go home and taking her in my arms and kissing her and then saying, "Oh, I'm so sorry." Apparently I was forgiven because of what happened not long after that.

I should mention that I graduated in June of 1929. I have no doubt; it is in the back of my mind, and it must be a fact, Wall Street heard I was coming, and so it collapsed in October 1929. That must be the cause. I see no other reason for it. When I graduated I had been working downtown on week-ends, part time, at the Credit Reference Exchange. This was a credit company that made reports of credit on people.

For instance, if you were a Chicagoan and you went to Miami and you wanted to open up a credit account in a store in Miami, maybe Marshall Field or Carson, Pirie, Scott, or Saks Fifth Avenue, you went to that store and filled out a form with your name and address and other information. The store then mailed your information to our credit bureau. Then we took those credit requests to the stores in Chicago that you are requesting credit from in Miami. I was called a runner. I went up and down Michigan Avenue and State Street in the Loop to all these various stores. Store personnel filled out what they knew about the person requesting the credit in Miami. Then I went back a few days later to pick up the forms and took them back to the Credit Reference Exchange. Three or four men were assigned to typing up the final reports for Miami. They showed whether or not you were good at paying your bills. And, of course, this was the business. They had files on thousands upon thousands of people in their files.

One of the men who worked there named Russell Dunlap was a little older than me, I imagine in his early thirties. He took a liking to me and we became friends at work. We palled around at work. One day he came to me and said, "Charlie, my girlfriend and I are going to drive to Crown Point, Indiana, and get married by a Justice of the Peace tonight. I had told him about Grace. He said, "Why don't you and Grace go with us and we'll get married at the same time. We'll have a double wedding." I thought, wow! Wow!

I went home and got hold of Grace and said, "Honey, Russell Dunlap suggested we go with him and his girlfriend tonight (I do not remember if it was that particular night or the following Saturday or something) and we'll have a double wedding at Crown Point. We'll get married secretly." We talked it over and decided we would do that. We made the date with Russell and at the appointed time we took off in his car. I did not have a car and did not drive.

On the way to Crown Point Russell and his girlfriend got into a heated exchange and decided not to get married. So, that left Grace and Charlie, who did get married. The Justice of the Peace questioned Grace because she looked like fifteen although she had recently turned eighteen. I was only twenty. I gave the Justice my birth date and he did not question me further. He performed the ceremony, pronounced us husband and wife, and gave us our marriage certificate. Russell drove us back to our respective parents' homes.

Three days later, now mind you, we are secretly married, she lives at home with her parents, I live at home with my parents, and three days later her mother and dad left on their vacation, taking their supposedly unmarried daughter with them for our honeymoon. So I always said, in the years to come, that Grace went on our honeymoon alone.

Remember, in 1929 the depression arose and men stood on corners trying to get jobs. They bought a crate of apples and sold them for five cents apiece, trying to make enough money to buy food for their families. It was an extremely rough time.

One day, after about a year and four months, Grace and I went down to the Embassy Theater to go to the show on Saturday. It was crowded. People were lined up waiting to get in. Well, you know, big time Charlie, he does not wait in line to go in to see a show. So then, what are we going to do?

Suddenly a bright light came to my mind. I said, "Honey, didn't your parents say they were going to be out of town today?"

"Yes," she said.

I said, "Why don't we go back to your place for a little time," and she agreed. So we did go there. Her mother, being a suspicious lady, came back suddenly, without warning, and rushed up the stairs to discover a commotion going on. We heard her coming up the stairs and tried to get ourselves together but she was fast!

Her mother came into her bedroom and raised particular havoc and called me all kinds of names, with rough language, and balled us out and I said to Grace, "Honey, go get our marriage certificate and show it to your mother," which she did. Well! That made her mother worse.

She said, "You're not going to live with us!" and she stormed out of the room and down the stairs. We thought our being married would calm her down.

In a few minutes we were ready, left her house, and went over to my mother's and dad's house.

We now have to tell my mother and dad about our marriage. We went in and quickly told my mother all about it. She said she was surprised but pleased, and said, "Now you're going to have to tell your father."

My mother was a sweet lady and always helpful to us. She did everything she could to help her boys. Grace said she married me for my mother. I can believe that.

Now I had to go in and tell my father about our marriage. I went into the front room where he was reading the newspaper and said, "Dad, I've got something to tell you."

"Humph."

My dad was not a man for a lot of speech. He was a quiet man but he said, "Humph."

So I said to him, "Um, I want you to know that Grace and I are married."

"Oh."

I said, "We've been married for a year and four months."

"Humph." And that was it as far as dad was concerned. He and my mother loved Grace and she became like a daughter to them. Eventually her mother became used to the idea and treated me like a son.

Then we found a place to live. You know, it is strange, I think it was Margaret Durkin who got us a little two room place down at 29 South Monroe Street. It was just south of Garfield Park, off of Madison Street in Chicago. It was a building with six apartments in it. Somebody had bought the building and divided each flat into smaller living areas. We had the kitchen and dining room in one of the apartments as our living space.

The kitchen was equipped with all the necessary things for cooking and it had a back porch outside the kitchen door. The dining room was now a bedroom with a double bed in it. This was our first love nest. We loved it. The price was $6 a week and we got linens furnished once a week. I paid $24 for the first month's rent, all the money I had.

I was not working at this time but Grace was working for A. B. Dick and Company, making $13 a week, so we had enough money coming in. On Sunday we bundled up our dirty clothes and took the streetcar to my parents' home. Grace did the laundry and we visited, and later went back home with clean clothes.

Grace and I spent hours across the street walking around in Garfield Park. It was a lovely park. You could walk, in those days, right into the evening. There were no gangs or mischief or that type of thing to worry about in the park. We went across the bridge onto the island and sat and spooned. We watched the moon come up and we were in love.

We went to the movie theater near our place, I forget the name of it now, but, we went there on Sundays nearly every week. In those days, also, there were other events taking place in our area. There was a roller derby that we used to go and watch. One time there was a "dance 'til you drop," dance in the park. Whoever danced the longest won a prize. We went to many events there.

When we were living there, my friend, Andrew Livingstone, one of the boys I grew up with on Belden Avenue, and palled around with most of the time, was a manager of a National Tea Store. Andy asked me if I wanted to work for him part time. I think it was two or three days a week. I agreed and I began earning $7.50 a week. With Grace's $13.00 and my $7.50 we had $20.00 bucks coming in every week, boy, we were rich.

I should mention, even in those early days, I was a gambler and I made bets on horse races. I often took fifty cents of the extra money I had and placed fifty cent bets on horses. I could always find a bookie. The disease of gambling was buried in me in those days. I was cautious about it. Grace knew nothing about it at that time. There was a time when I needed to pay money I owed but I did not have it. My dad and mom bailed me out but that was a mistake because I went right back into it.

Shortly after I began working at the National Tea, Andy's manager came to me and asked if I would like to manage a National Tea Store full time. I jumped at that chance. Oh yes, I sure would I told him. He took me over to a little store on Pulaski Road just north of Chicago Avenue, about six blocks down. This little store was doing $450 worth of business a week, and it was in the red. This was in March.

I had one girl working for me and we did all the work. We set up the supplies, stocked the shelves and I did the ordering. We waited on customers over the counter. Everything was run by the two of us. There was no such thing as self-serve or taking things off the shelves yourself and going up to the cashier to pay for them. If a lady came in and wanted a loaf of bread, we got it and placed it on the counter, and then we sold her a pound of butter to go with the loaf of bread. If she wanted a steak dinner we reminded her we had canned corn and canned peas on sale, and asked her how many cans she wanted. I had stacked the cans up in a prominent place with a "sale" sign on them.

My manager was a sharp man. He came into the store and said to me, "Next week we're having a big sale on #2 cans of corn at seven cents a can. How many cases shall I order for you?"

I thought it through; well now, this is on sale, and I recalled about how many cans we usually sold and figured how many more people would buy if it was on sale, and I said, "I can probably use four cases."

"That's fine. I'll send you six cases," he said.

Shrewd Charlie, here, he caught on to this trick and so later on, when the boss came in and said, "How many cases can you use," I told him we could use two cases.

"I'll send you four cases," he said, which is what Charlie wanted in the first place.

I managed that store for a year. I brought it up to $650 a week in business. The boss came in one day and said, "I'm going to transfer you to another store, if you agree. It's about six blocks south of here at Augusta and Pulaski. It's doing $650 worth of business, a bigger store, and I'm going to give you a $3 a week raise." He was paying me

$15 a week for sixty hour weeks. With this promotion to a larger store I would earn $18 a week. So I hurried home to tell Grace of my great promotion and the next week I took over the second store at $650 a week in sales. A year later I was doing $850 a week in that store and going along well.

I got word from my dad in 1935 that the Chicago Surface Lines was going to hire streetcar conductors. They paid seventy-eight cents an hour. The schedule was that a motorman or conductor worked seven days a week and then got a day off. For instance, he worked seven days and was off on Monday. Then he worked the next seven days and was off on Tuesday. Whenever the off day fell on Saturday, he had Saturday and Sunday off.

I went downtown to the Chicago Surface Lines headquarters on Lake Street to put in an application. Someone had told me that they liked to hire people whose parents had been on the job in the past, and if they took your picture, you had a pretty good chance of getting called. I filled out the application and was turned over to the interviewer. He asked me why I wanted to be a streetcar conductor and I said, "I think I would enjoy the work, and my dad was on the streetcars for six years."

"Oh, he was?" he said.

"Yes," I said.

"Who was he?"

"Carl spelled with a "C" by the way, Carl Christensen." The interviewer handed me over to the photographer and he took my picture. I went home excited. They took my picture! That was a good sign.

It was a year later when I received a letter from them stating that if I was still interested in working for them I should come downtown to headquarters for a new interview.

I went in for that interview and they hired me on the spot. I put in my resignation as manager of the National Tea Company store.

Now as I said, I was making $18 a week at the National Tea. On the Chicago Surface Lines, working on a regular basis, I would make approximately $35 a week. When my boss at National Tea asked why I was leaving, I told him, "Because I can make double the salary working there."

STARTING A FAMILY AND AS A STREETCAR CONDUCTOR

I was hired by the Chicago Surface Lines as a streetcar conductor beginning January 9, 1936. They had not hired anybody since 1933.

I was an extra man. As an extra man I was put on call at 4:00 o'clock in the morning. At the Western Avenue and Division Street depot I was the first one on call each night at 4:00 a.m. Then there was an extra man at 4:15 and another at 4:30 and a man at 4:45 and one at 5:00 o'clock. If a full time worker did not come in to begin his run on time, the supervisor took the run away from him and gave it to an extra man. The full-timer went to the back of the line as an extra man for that day. Or, if a man called in sick, then I took his run. Nobody behind me went to work unless I went to work. There were days when I went in at 4:00 o'clock, and the extra men piled up behind me and eventually it was 8:00 a.m. and not one extra man had been given a run. No runs became available that night.

Many of us knew each other and liked to play games. Sometimes a half dozen of us would go to one's home, not my home, where we played poker. One of us would make a little bit of money if he got lucky. Or, there were times when we took what little money we had and went to the racetrack to play the horses. Play the horses. Play the horses. This was a great, sad, time in my life.

Grace and I, when our income got a little better, moved to a little five room basement flat at 1936 North Keystone Avenue. We were living there when I got my job on the Chicago Surface Lines. We had been married three-and-a-half years.

Grace became pregnant shortly after we moved there. When the baby decided it was time to arrive, my mother and I went with Grace to Franklin Boulevard Hospital. Dr. Choinard was our doctor. Now he was a doctor! He made house calls and he charged only three dollars. House calls! And if you did not happen to pay him when he came, he never asked for the money or sent a bill. He was a fantastic man.

We were in the hospital that evening with Grace settled into a room when he came to see her. She was having a pain here and a pain there but he examined her and came out to where my mother and I were waiting and said, "Mr. Christensen, my advice to you is to go home and spend the evening getting a good rest. Your wife is not going to have this baby tonight."

I went in to Grace's room to talk with her. I explained to her what the doctor had said, "But," I said, "I'll stay with you."

"No," she said, "you go home and get a good night's rest."

"Okay," I said, and Mother and I went home. At 5:30 in the morning I got a telephone call. The doctor wanted me to come to the hospital. Mom and I quickly got ready and hopped on the streetcars, the Armitage car over to Kedzie and the Kedzie car down to Franklin Boulevard and then we walked the rest of the way to the Franklin Boulevard Hospital. When we entered the reception area, one of the nurses said, "You need to go up to the third floor. Doc is waiting for you. He wants to talk to you."

We had to walk up those three floors and my knees were shaking. I was scared. What was happening? Why does the doctor want to see me? Why is it so hard to have a baby? We arrived at Dr. Choinard's office and he quickly explained that his purpose for wanting to talk to me was that he had to use forceps to help the delivery and he needed my consent. I gave my consent, what do I know, I was sure the doctor knew what he was doing so Rae Ann came forth with a little help with forceps. And there was our beautiful baby girl. Rae Ann was born on February 18, 1936. We had been married in 1932 in August and this was our first lovely girl.

Two years later I knew what to expect when Deanne was born on January 10. And so we had two lovely daughters.

I do not know how old the girls were but they were still very young, maybe one and three years old when we moved to 4859 North Bernard Street. It was a basement apartment, five rooms, right across the street from a Jewish Synagogue. Across the other street there was a Jewish old people's home. This was a mostly Jewish neighborhood. We liked our place. We got along well with our neighbors.

Grace sewed dresses for herself and the two girls. She made matching outfits including little hats and some with intricate embroidery work. She was quite a seamstress.

The man who lived in the flat upstairs owned a yard goods store and sometimes he brought fabrics home and gave them to Grace. She took out a pattern and sewed up something and later took it upstairs to show it to him. He brought home a nice crepe fabric that Grace sewed into blouses with cap sleeves and decorated with individual sequins and beads in a swirling pattern. They were absolutely gorgeous and she was able to sell quite a few of these blouses for a hefty sum. Our upstairs neighbor was completely amazed at her work. He was a very sweet man. He was awfully nice to us.

Grace had to do a lot of sewing. I brought most of my money home but because of my gambling I always accumulated gambling debts. I could go to any one of three loan sharks, walk into the office and say I need money, and I could sign my name and get any amount I wanted up to $800. I always owed $400, or $600 up to $800 to these fellows and I made payments. If I could not make a payment I called and said I wanted to pay only the interest. Now the interest was three percent per month so it was a high interest, I suppose, in those days. I did not think of this as evil. This was a part of the excitement in life for me, my motive in my mind was to win a bundle and buy things for my family. Of course these were phony motives. Always phony, supposedly good desires in this terrible thing that I did. So that was part of my life.

FROM STREETCAR CONDUCTOR TO BUS DRIVER

I was on the streetcars from 1936 to 1946 when the Chicago Surface Lines, later the Chicago Transit Authority, (CTA,) began converting to busses. I was told to convert from being a streetcar conductor to driving a bus.

The CTA subsequently closed that Western Avenue and Division Street depot, sold it to the city, I guess, because the city then built this huge high school on that property. It was named San Clemente High after a famous ball player named Roberto Clemente. He died in an airplane crash on December 31, 1971. He had played with the Pittsburg Pirates.

I had worked out of the Western and Division Street depot for only a short time, less than a year, when I was moved up and off the extra list and was able to pick a run. Of course, I was on the bottom of the scale and I got only what was left. However, there were times when a lot of the conductors would not work with certain men for various reasons although the run might be a good one.

Division – Western April 1949

One of these men was Old Diamond Johnny. He worked nights on Division Street, a short run from California Street at 2800 west, going east down to Wells Street, which was 200 west, a 26 block run. The run made two round trips from California to Wells and then it ran ten round trips from California to Milwaukee Avenue which was 2800 west down to 1600 west a matter of a mile-and-a-half, perhaps. That was Diamond Johnny's night run. He was called Old Diamond Johnny because he wore diamonds; imagine wearing them on the streetcar and never getting robbed.

Old Diamond Johnny was an old grouch. But it was a good, soft run, and it paid well. Our runs were paid eight hours. If you worked over time, you got time-and-a-half. (In my last fifteen years on the job, when I was driving busses, I picked up a nine hour and six-tenths wage on a daily run, five days a week which gave me a forty-eight hour work week. In those days we were making $6.69 an hour. That is when I quit the job back in 1974. I was making $6.69 an hour.)

Western Avenue was the longest straight transportation run in Chicago. It was twenty-two miles from Howard Street at 7600 north to 119th Street on the south, one straight run. I made one round trip run to 119th and one round trip run from 7600 north to 79th Street south and that was my day's work. I liked working that run.

I picked that very nice, well-paying run, which I worked with a man who was called, Ova da Road Berglund. Berglund was a Swede and he would never run ahead of time. Now, mind you, streetcars ran every minute-and-a-half. Almost every time the light changed, a streetcar would go by with two men on it. There was a motorman and a conductor, and we were loaded in rush trips. Sometimes passengers hung out the back end of the streetcar. If you did not keep your distance between the guy ahead of you, if he ran a minute ahead of time, on a minute-and-a-half headway, that gave you a two-and-a-half minute headway behind him unless you watched out for yourself and moved up a minute to hold your own time distance behind him.

Ova Da Road Berglund was a very honest motorman. If the car ahead of him ran a minute ahead of schedule that meant more passengers were gathering at the bus stops for us to pick up and that meant more fare collecting for me as conductor. But, it was a good run and I liked Berglund, so I picked the run to work with Ova Da Road Berglund.

Now Over Da Road Berglund played checkers and he was a whiz. This was a day run; we worked straight through, so we could go into the barn to have our time off for lunch.

We went into the barn, I guess it was almost the first day we worked together, and he said, "Let's play checkers." And so we sat down to play. I never even progressed into the king row, ever, playing with Ova Da Road. He wiped me off the board. I played with him for six months and every once in a while, during the last month or so, I acquired a king. But I could not win. I played with Ova Da Road Berglund that entire "pick," referring to the run I had "picked." One time I played a game to the draw and considered myself a champion. Charlie played Ova Da Road Berglund to a tie! I never did win.

Now there was one other thing at Western and Division Street I should mention. At the beginning of a streetcar run the motorman and conductor had to go out into the barn where the streetcars had been driven over pits. This was so the mechanics could get down into the pits to work on the underneath of the cars. We boarded the streetcar in the barn and prepared it for the passengers. We turned the seats around properly, facing front, and we put the electrical pole up on the wire from which we got power to move, and so on and so forth.

There was a man named Pedersen who worked out of this barn. He was called "The Preacher" and all of us young fellows used to kid him and make a lot of fun about The Preacher. I would come in and say, "Hey, Chris, Pedersen's out in the car pits. He's in his streetcar praying for us sinners," and we laughed at "The Preacher," and made fun of him. I never thought a thing about that. It was just fun. I never gave any thought to spiritual things.

Many, many years later, as a Christian, I went to a meeting somewhere, I forget what kind of a meeting, and met a man named Pedersen. As I was talking with him I said, "I don't suppose your father could have ever worked on the streetcars.

He looked surprised and said, "Oh, yes, he did work on the streetcars at Western and Division Streets many years before he retired."

"Wow," I said. "I knew your father. I worked out of that same barn. Would you mind telling him something for me?"

He said, "What's that?"

I said, "Tell him that one of his co-workers, who used to make sport of him because he was a Christian and preached the gospel, who used to laugh along with the rest of the men, is now a Christian. Tell him that the seed he planted, although he didn't know it at the time, must have taken root. I am now a saved man, at the age of thirty-nine, and it could be that his prayer was the beginning of my salvation. I want your father to know that although I made fun of him back then, that I thank him now for preaching the gospel. Will you do that?" and he said he would. And I thanked the Lord for that later. It was certainly a blessing to me.

THE ONE TERRIBLE ACCIDENT

I had an excellent accident record on streetcars and busses as a conductor and driver, but I was involved in one accident while on my way to work on a Western Avenue streetcar. We were two blocks north of where I had to get off at Division Street to go to work. I was standing on the front platform against the heater that was right behind where the motorman stood to drive the streetcar. I had my hands behind me on the heater. It was in March, and it was cold. There was a man standing to the left of the motorman in the corner of the platform and a third man standing on the other side by the front door waiting to get off when we got down to Division Street.

First I should explain about how the streetcars reversed directions. When we got to the end of the line the platforms at each end of the car were swapped from motorman to conductor and from conductor to motorman. In other words, the front of the car was converted into the rear and vice versa. The platform where the motorman stood had doors that folded closed behind him and a bar lay across those doors. There were little bitty holes that the metal bar fit down into. While the motorman was driving, that bar was set into place behind him to keep passengers out of his way. So when we switched ends we removed the bar from behind the motorman and set it into holes where it was stored and then the conductor used that space to collect fares. I was standing in the front end and we were heading south on Western Avenue. I saw a five ton truck passing a north bound streetcar a block down the street ahead of us and it was coming toward us on our rails. He passed up that streetcar and cut in front of it but instead of straightening out on his side of the street; he cut back across to our rails again and ran head on into our streetcar.

There is a four foot beam on each corner of the streetcar that holds up the framework. One of those corner beams was smashed in from the impact and a piece of lumber pierced the thigh of the man who had been standing in the corner waiting to get off. I believe he was hurt worse than I was. It was a serious accident.

As for me, the bar that went across those doors was knocked up and out of its retaining holes and thrown at me hitting me in the back of the head. Also, the windows in the front of the streetcar blew in and cut a huge gash across my cheek and another on my forehead. I had tried to hold on to those little holes that the reversing bar fit down into but I did not make it. That bar came up and hit me, and I got cut by flying glass, plus I lost my hat.

We were only a block from the depot where the boss, if he stood up at his desk, could see down Western. He heard the crash and saw what happened and called the fire department. They were there within a minute-and-a-half, I think, because they were only a block away. I was lying on the platform and a fireman came over and kneeled down beside me and said, "Lay still Chris, we're going to help you, just lay still, it will be all right, don't try to get up."

I said, "Where's my hat. I want my hat. My hat fell off." You see, my badge was on my hat. If I lost my badge, I would lose a day's work until I could get it replaced. So I did not want to lose my badge. Someone grabbed my hat and handed it to me and I guess that was all right then, but I was in a daze.

The police took me to St. Mary's Hospital, just off of Division Street, a couple of blocks east of the barn, put me in a wheel chair and then they began asking me questions. They wanted to know how I felt. I said, "I'm sick, I don't feel good." Then the hospital people took me upstairs somewhere to get a head scan. Apparently, they thought I had a concussion although it turned out I did not have one.

The only thing that upset me later was that this other fellow got hauled off to the hospital on a fire truck and they threw me in a paddy wagon. (Police car)

For the following six months, on occasion, I would be combing my hair and cut my finger on a piece of glass that had come out of my head. Then I had to go back to the doctor and have him pull it out with a pair of tweezers. I was off work for three or four weeks on sick leave, but the company did not send my sick pay check to me. I kept asking for it but they still did not send it. Finally I called up the union and complained that the company would not send me my sick pay. I had to literally sue the company to get that check. I do not know if the lawsuit went on my record, but I got my bills paid and it was finally settled. Later on I transferred up to Clark Street, to the depot north of Devon Avenue.

MY LIFE CHANGED IN A SECOND

I am going to jump ahead a little bit, here. At this point in my life I had transferred away from the Western and Division Depot up to Clark Street. I was now a bus driver. I had been on the job for fifteen years. Grace and I had been married for nineteen years, Rae Ann was 15 years of age, Deanne was 13 years old, (Christine was not yet born) and I was deeply into my gambling business, almost daily.

It was a hidden part of my life, although not entirely hidden. A couple of times I had confessed the gambling and really strove to set myself straight but invariably I went back to it. I would pay off my debts, and get out, and then drift back again and it just seemed to be something that was uncontrollable, it was in me, it was part of my being, and I had no thought of anything wrong with it.

I was a good husband. I did not chase women, I did not drink. Grace and I went to parties, occasionally, with a group of friends that gathered together down at the Division Street Depot. There were, perhaps, half a dozen couples of streetcar men and their wives who got together every third Saturday. There was dancing, food, drinking, and playing poker, and maybe at two o'clock in the morning a change over from poker to shooting craps.

We won and lost money that we never had, and if I went broke, I borrowed ten bucks from another buddy, or if he went broke, I loaned him ten bucks and it was all a part of life.

Grace was aware of the gambling. She knew I gambled but she did not know a lot of the dirty details of when I went to the loan sharks to borrow money. This, too, was part of my life.

There was a family story later on of how Grace did learn about these loan sharks and became extremely angry at them. The story goes that she got herself together and went to several of them and told them off. She told them they had better not loan me any more money or she would . . . I don't know what she threatened, or if it had any effect on the loan sharks, but this is the feisty woman I married. I love her deeply.

We lived in the 2800 block of Wellington Avenue at that time, just east of California Avenue. We were there ten years. We had moved from the Jewish neighborhood on Bernard, to that little four-flat and then we lived here for ten years in the six-flat. The girls went to Brentano Grammar School in those days.

There was a lady that we knew; the mother-in-law of one of my fellow bus drivers, who asked if she could take our girls to Sunday school at the Maplewood Avenue Baptist Church. I had no fault with that. She picked the girls up, took them to Sunday school, and brought them back home again. I did not pay any attention to that and I do not remember how long that went on.

Years later I noticed my daughter, Rae Ann, who was fifteen years old at this time, bowing her head before we ate our meals. I did not pay too much attention but I wondered what was going on. She had been going to Mayfair Bible Church for some months and I was a bit concerned that she was getting into something that I knew nothing about.

The assistant pastor of the church and his wife, Clem and Marie Bilhorn, who lived close to where we lived, picked her up and took her to Sunday school and church. They lived in a house across the street from Rae Ann's grammar school, where a couple of ladies, Miss Olds and Miss Utley, provided a place for people to live as they studied for the ministry. Miss Olds and Miss Utley ran a children's club, almost like a daily vacation bible school, on a permanent basis and Rae Ann had been a club member while attending Brentano. Anyway, Clem and his wife were living there and taking Rae Ann to Mayfair Bible Church which was up at Wilson Avenue, just east of Cicero Avenue.

When I asked Rae Ann what she was doing when she bowed her head before meals she told us she was thanking God for providing the food she and our family needed.

Then she began the story of what had occurred when she had attended a High-C Rally, a Youth for Christ type rally. This was a huge gathering of Christian young people of high school age. She had attended with her friend, Dale Haupers. She told us a man named Gregorio Tingson had preached about how Jesus Christ had died for our sins. She said Mr. Tingson talked about how Jesus is the Son of God and that He was crucified on a cross, was buried, but that He rose up from the dead. He was seen by over five hundred people, and later was caught up into heaven to be with His father. She told us this and said Jesus died so that we could be forgiven of our sin and to have peace with God. She said we could invite Him into our hearts to be our Savior, and the Lord of our lives. I had no understanding of any of this.

I was not interested in any of it. But she told us she had received Jesus Christ as her Savior and I was concerned she was caught up in a cult.

Rae Ann came home one day and said to mom and me, "Daddy, would it be all right if I brought some young people home with me after the evening service at church for what we call an after meeting?"

I thought well, yeah, I do not see anything wrong with that. Besides then, maybe, I could see what was going on with this group from church and so I said, "You can have an after meeting here if you want to. Invite the young people over. I'll get some pop and cookies."

At nine o'clock that particular Sunday evening the doorbell rang in our little four-room flat on the second floor. I pushed the button to allow our visitors into the hallway and here came these kids up the stairwell. Forty-two young people, plus Clem Bilhorn, marched into my living room and sat around in a circle on the floor. They sang hymns and choruses, songs praising the Lord, for an hour-and-a-half. Now I was not paying a great deal of attention to the songs, however, their singing made an impression on me.

Clem came out into the kitchen where Grace and I were sitting. We had one of those doors that swings back and forth as you go through it. We closed this door after Clem came out to sit at the kitchen table to visit with us. He did not preach at us that I recall. We talked about normal life, about the church, things that the kids did, and all this time the kids were in the front room singing and giving testimonies. I did not know what giving testimonies was at that time but later learned it meant talking about how the Lord had helped them in their lives and kept them doing right. All of the fun and joy that came out of those kids apparently touched me in my heart without my even realizing it. The fun broke up around 10:30 p.m. and they left.

I do not remember exactly when Rae Ann was saved in 1951, very early in the year, I'm sure. (February 23) Anyway, early in that year she came to ask me to go to Sunday school with her or just to church. Rae Ann would say, "Daddy, will you go to church with me?" and I would say, "Oh, no, no, no, I'm not going to go, I'm not interested in church. You go to church."

She would come again a week or so later and say, "Daddy, won't you please go to church with me?"

"No, no," I said, "I don't want to go to church. I told you I did not want to go to church. You go to church. Just leave me alone."

A week would go by, Rae Ann was back. "Daddy, will you go to church with me next Sunday."

"Now, I told you I didn't want to go to church. I told you to leave me alone and if you don't quit bugging me I'm not going to let you go either," and I said, "Quit pestering me! Do you understand?"

"Yes Daddy," she said rather sadly.

"Okay." So I had won that battle. But the Lord was at work.

I think two or three weeks went by, the time element in here is vague. But, sometime before Easter Rae Ann came to me one day and said, "Daddy, I have something very important to tell you."

And I said, "Fine, what is it?"

She said, "You have to promise me you won't get angry."

I said, "No, I won't get angry," I said, "What do you want to tell me?"

"No, you have to promise me you will not get angry with me first," she insisted.

I was a man of the world. I had been a CTA bus driver for fifteen years. I was thirty-nine years old. I had two daughters and now here is one coming to me wanting to talk to me and I am wondering what is going on here, and hoping it was nothing too serious. My mind, worldly as it was, began getting a little fretful. So I said to her, "Okay, I won't get mad at you. What do you want to tell me?"

She said, "Daddy I know you're going to church!"

Here we are back to that again. I said, "Oh? How do you know that?"

"Because we've been praying for you and Mom and God answers prayer," she responded. She said it quite convincingly however I did not want to hear that.

"Well," I said, "We'll see about that."

I do not know how much time went by after that until she came to me a week before Easter Sunday and said, "Daddy, will you please go to Easter Sunday service with me?"

That was the top off. I blasted at her. I did not swear at her, I did not use cursing language. I was not a man to swear. If I got upset and very angry and lost control, I could swear with the best of men. Foul language, however, was not used in my parents' home and so I did not develop that habit. But, I yelled at her, "I told you not to bother me about this," and I got very upset and told her off and she said "Sorry, Daddy," and she quit.

Grace came to me that same evening and said, "You know, if you loved your daughter, you'd go to church if it would make her happy." She said, "It wouldn't hurt you to go to church for one Sunday. It might hurt the church but it won't hurt you. Deanne and I are going to go with Rae Ann next Sunday." Now Grace was not a church attendee or a Christian. She did not have any religion, so to speak, at all, that I was aware of.

And so, when she said this I said, "All right. Okay. I'll go to church with her on Easter Sunday if it'll make her happy. But, if she comes back to me and says, see, Daddy, I told you, I knew you were going to go to church, I'll slap her up agin the wall." Of course, I didn't really mean I would slap her. That was just a figure of speech of mine.

Grace, smart woman that she is, cautioned Rae Ann, "If we go to church, don't say I told you so to Daddy."

We went Easter Sunday. The Pastor preached, I listened, and we went on our way home, mind you, on streetcars because we did not have a car. We walked east about three-quarters of a mile and got on an Elston Avenue streetcar and rode down to Wellington Avenue, got off and walked to our apartment four blocks away. On the way home, Rae Ann said, "Well, Daddy, what did you think of the service?"

"Eh," I said, "It was okay. The man's a good talker." Pastor Charles Bartels was pastor of the church, a humble, Godly man who knew the Bible and its doctrines well. I did not know this at that time, but it proved itself out.

It was about three weeks later, on a Saturday evening when Grace came to me and said, "By the way." Grace knew how to approach people. She said, "By the way. I am going to Sunday school and church tomorrow with the girls. I don't know whether you want to go or not, but I'm going."

I looked at her and said, "Okay. I'll go with you." Then I thought *why in the world did I say a dumb thing like that?* I did not want to go to Sunday school and church. Sunday school is for kids. But, you know, Grace and me, even though I had this bad habit of gambling, we were in love. I loved my wife and she loved me, in spite of my faults, she loved me. And we always did everything, down through the years, together, with the kids. So we went to church together. The first was that Easter Sunday in 1951 and three weeks later we began attending Sunday school and church on a regular basis.

On June 22, 1951 Rae Ann led her sister, Deanne, who was thirteen, to the Lord in the bathroom of our apartment while they were fixing their hair. You know how girls are, they were puttering around in the bathroom and they began talking about the Lord. Deanne and her friend, Pat, decided to accept Jesus as their Savior and so Rae Ann prayed with them to do that.

I was not aware of this when we went to church the following Sunday, the 24th of June, 1951. There were, perhaps, two-hundred-and-fifty people in the church auditorium. I was sitting about two-thirds of the way back, in the pew seat closest to the center aisle. Grace sat right next to me and the girls were farther toward the front on the other side of the center aisle.

Pastor preached on two verses. The first was II Corinthians 5:17 which reads, "Therefore, if any man be in Christ, he is a new creature. Old things are passed away, behold, all things are become new." (KJV) He also preached from II Corinthians 8:12 which reads, "If there first be a willing mind, it is accepted according to that a man hath, and not according to that he hath not." (KJV) At the end of the service, the people in the church began singing a hymn. It is an invitational hymn, *While on Others Thou Art Calling, Do Not Pass Me By,* and the pastor gave an invitation to anyone who did not know Jesus as his Savior, to come to the altar where someone could pray with him and show him how to accept this new life that was offered by God.

While this was going on, Rae Ann and Deanne left their pew and walked down the aisle to join the Pastor at the altar. Deanne had decided she wanted to make a public profession to the congregation the she had accepted Jesus Christ as her Savior.

What happened next was totally amazing. Two hundred and fifty people were in the church. I was standing three quarters of the way back at the seat next to the aisle, Grace was next to me, and while the people sang that hymn, I felt as though I were totally alone in the auditorium. There was a voice, so to speak, on my right hand saying, *Charlie, come to me. I will give you a new life. Old things are going to pass away. You can have a new life in me that will be full and rich.* This astounding invitation was there. The thought of beginning over again, of getting rid of the old way of life that was causing my heart to stress, keeping me in misery all the time, appealed to me in a huge way.

But, I owed a thousand dollars in gambling debts that Grace did not even know about at this moment.

On my other side, there was another voice, seemingly saying, *do not be a chump. Do not go forward, do not move, fellow. If you go down there, you know what is going to happen. You are going to have to tell Grace about your gambling debt.* The voice seemed to say you are going to lose your family. Do not be a fool. Stay where you are, and I was nailed, emotionally nailed, to the floor. I could not move. But, the wooing of the Lord and the Holy Spirit's call to come to Jesus was beginning to overpower me. I had been attending this church long enough to have heard much Scripture although I did not know any verses from the Bible.

47

Beginning anew appealed to my heart and my mind. Satan did everything he could to keep me from going forward. And, it was true, he had me emotionally nailed to the floor, I could not step forward.

Out of the clear, without any warning whatsoever, I got a poke in my side by an elbow. The elbow was attached to Grace Minerva Christensen. She said, "Move over. I'm going forward," and as she stepped past me into the aisle I lifted up my hand and said, "Wait for me," and I was loosed from the nails on the floor and I went down the aisle with Grace and kneeled at the altar next to her and my daughters.

After the service, as the congregation was leaving, Pastor Bartels took us back into the prayer room and began explaining what my actions meant. Someone else was speaking to Grace, I believe, and Deanne was with her. Rae Ann was with me. Pastor Bartels asked if I understood what was preached. I said, "Well, I know you preached about a new life. I don't know any Scripture but you said," and he had me read it from his Bible, "Therefore, if any man be in Christ, he is a new creature, old things are passed away, behold all things become new." (KJV)

He said, "Do you believe you are a sinner?"

"Oh, yes," I said. "I know I'm a sinner."

He said, "Would you be willing to taste and see that the Lord is good? Would you be willing to invite Jesus Christ to come into your heart to be your Savior from sin?"

"Well, yes. I would like to do that." I said, "But I don't know how to do it."

He said, "You just pray to God."

I said, "I don't know how to pray."

He said, "You talk to God the same as you are talking to me. You tell God that you realize you're a sinner, you ask

Him to forgive you and you invite his precious Son to come into your heart to be your savior from sin. And, if you mean business with God, Jesus said, "Behold I stand at the door and knock. If any man hear my voice and will open the door, I will come into him." And so I prayed what is called the sinner's prayer. I said, "God, I don't know what this is all about but I want it. I know I'm a sinner. I confess myself a sinner to you and I want to invite Jesus Christ to come into my heart to be my Savior from sin." I do not remember inviting him in to be the Lord of my life at that point.

It happened. Do not ask a man who has just accepted Christ what happened. The transition is from God. It is divine. Christ enters the heart by the Holy Spirit and he is renewed. If you have ever read *Pilgrim's Progress* you will recall the pilgrim had a great weight on his back. But the time came when he received a savior and that weight fell off. That weight fell off my back. When I got up on my feet I knew something had happened. I was at peace with myself. It was a great burden lifted from me.

I then realized there was still the time to come when I had to tell Grace about my gambling. She was accepting Christ at the same time I was with the guidance of one of the other ministers of the church. I don't know if it was a man or a woman. We went home that morning as true believers in Jesus Christ. The whole family had been born into the family of God. Of course, the confession about my gambling debts was extremely difficult for me but mostly for Grace. We cried and prayed and she graciously forgave me and eventually I paid off all that I owed the loan sharks. Our new lives in Christ had begun.

BEGINNING EFFECTS
OF LIFE CHANGES

The very next day, on Monday night, I went to pick up my bus, and when I walked into the depot Joe came up to me and said, "Hey, Chris. We got a hot one tomorrow running in the fourth race." He meant he thought they had the name of a racehorse that was sure to win and he wanted me to bet on it with the bookies.

I said, "Joe, I'm sorry, I can't play it."

"Well, what's the matter Chris," he said, "you broke?" he said, "I'll lend you a sawbuck." ($10 bill)

"No," I said, "It's not the money part of it. I accepted Jesus Christ as my Savior yesterday and He has delivered me from gambling. I cannot gamble anymore."

The word got around the depot quickly and my co-workers began calling me The Deacon. Later on they called me The Preacher, and eventually, I wound up with the name Preacher and for the next twenty-three years I preached Jesus on my bus. Even the boss called me Preacher. If I got called into the office for an infraction of rules the boss would say, "What are you doing in here, Preacher?" I realized I had to set an example and praise God, I was able to witness and talk about Jesus. I kept gospel tracks on my bus and

I witnessed to people openly and loudly. I talked to other drivers as I had a chance. I led one bus driver to Jesus right there in the depot while we were all writing up our runs one night. Drivers picked a run, and filled in the paperwork, and then went out to their busses to prepare them for the night's work. I talked about the Lord at these times and I had many opportunities of doing that.

This was really the beginning. I had been married nineteen years. Our family consisted of a man, thirty-nine years old, a woman thirty-seven years old, two teen-aged daughters, and we were now a born again family. We continued attending Mayfair Bible Church together for many years beginning in 1951. My daughter, Christine, was born on September 22, 1952 and she began church attendance as a baby.

My burden, immediately, was for kids. I wanted kids to come to Jesus Christ and not have to wait until the age of thirty-nine to find out the reality of who Jesus is. I became an AWANA (Approved Workmen Are Not Ashamed) youth leader. I was the Sunday school bus driver; I became the Sunday school superintendent. I became president of the Men's Over-Forty Fellowship. I was this and I was that, in fact, I became extremely busy for the Lord and in His work.

I finished my bus driving at 5:30 in the morning. Clem Bilhorn often came out to Gompers Park on Foster Avenue to run five miles at 6:00 a.m. and we would meet there. He would run, I would walk, and then we would sit and pray. We would pray for young people in the youth work. Clem was our youth pastor and I was a leader in our AWANA Club and we prayed for individuals and studied the Bible together. It was a blessed time.

When the AWANA Clubs began at North Side Gospel Center in Chicago, I was blessed to be able to help Pastor Lance Latham mimeograph the lessons and then distribute them to local churches. My house on Irving Park Road was just around the corner from this church. The AWANA clubs are an international Christian organization, serving children.

As a leader in our church's AWANA Club I went to church on Monday evening dressed in my bus driver's uniform. I had bought a car in 1955 so around 8:15 p.m. I had to run and jump in my car and drive to the depot to begin my night shift. I drove a bus for nine-and-a-half hours and then met Clem in Gompers Park on Foster Avenue in the morning. I had energy and I was on the go. My problem was that I was so busy <u>for</u> the Lord that I did not seem to have much time <u>with</u> the Lord, personally. Everybody thought *what a fine tremendous Christian Charlie Christensen is*. Everybody patted me on the back.

That went on for perhaps two-and-a-half years. I was into everything at church and then one day one of the men at the barn came up to me and said, "Hey, Chris, we got a hot one tomorrow. You wanna play it?"

"Ah, come on, Joe, you know I don't play the horses anymore."

"I know, I was only teasing," he said. "I thought you might wanna play it."

I said, "Who is it?" These were the worst words I ever said in my life. "Who is it?"

"Well, so and so in the fifth race."

I had paid off all my gambling debts, I did not owe anything, and now I put my hand in my pocket and came up with two dollars, and said, "Joe, put two dollars to win on it for me, will you?"

Well (sigh) Satan always comes back to a weak spot. If he cannot get a Christian's soul into hell he will do all he can to break him down in his testimony and his life. And I began, once again, betting on the ponies. The next thing I knew, I was fifty dollars into the bookie. Well, that was no problem. I went to the loan shark and borrowed a hundred bucks and paid off the bookie. I used the other fifty to make another bet. I just knew I could win my money back again to pay off the loan, but it did not work that way. It never did. I wound up eighteen hundred dollars in the hole in the course of a couple of years. And, of course, it was building up in me. I was, of all men, most miserable. I was smiling and praising God and witnessing and doing this evil in my heart and the Lord allowed me to do it until he finally said that is enough Charlie.

After our salvation we moved out to Irving Park Road in 1951. Or, maybe it was early 1952. We lived there for eighteen years.

I came home one day, maybe three weeks before my breakdown and went down into our basement. I was so under conviction! I wrote a letter of confession to Grace. I said I loved her, I was sorry that I had allowed this to come back into my life, and that I was extremely distraught. But then I buried the letter downstairs. I hid it.

Three weeks later I came home from work at around six o'clock in the morning. Grace was up and I sat down at the counter to have coffee and toast with her. She looked at me and said, "Daddy . . .," By that time, being married all those years it was Daddy and Mommy, "Daddy, are you gambling again?"

That broke the dam and I wept. And I said "Yes. I've written you a letter that tells you all about it. I'll go downstairs and get it. I have it in the basement."

She said, "Can't you tell me to my face?"

I said, "No, I can't."

I gave her the letter and went out and got in my car and began driving. I do not know why I did this, but I drove to church. Nobody was there. I went downstairs into the new section where we had six different Sunday school rooms off to the side of a large gymnasium room and I went into one of those rooms and laid down on the cement floor and wept my heart out in remorse.

Now the Bartels lived on the grounds in the parsonage behind the church. Pastor Bartels used to come around outside the front of the building and go over to the side door into the older part of the church. I was in a newer section that had been added on. But he used to go all the way around, go up the outside stairs and into his office in the old church.

For some reason, that morning, he came in the front entrance of the new building to get to his office and as he did so he heard me weeping in that Sunday school room. He came in. "Charlie. Brother, what is the problem?"

I could hardly speak but I confessed to him my sinfulness, what I had done, that I had told Grace, and Charlie wept as though he were guilty of my sin and he prayed for me. (This entire story is told in tears as Dad recorded it years later.)

I went home and thought, well, I live right around the corner from the North Side Gospel Center which had started the AWANA Clubs, a great gospel preaching church, and I thought I will go over there and start anew on the Christian approach to my life. And then I read in Proverbs, "A brother *offended is harder to win than a walled city."* I thought what are you trying to tell me, Lord? And the Lord said to my mind, you lost a battle at Mayfair Bible Church but I'm going to win the war for you there. Go back to Mayfair.

So that week I went before the Board of the church and resigned all the offices that I held within the church. I said to those Godly men that I would understand if they wanted to take away my membership. After much prayer they decided not to do that.

For the next two years I attended Mayfair as a member of the church without office. I had no responsibility of service. At the end of two years they asked me if I would be assistant Sunday school superintendent again. And I said, "I'll pray about it."

It was a rough, extremely rough, time for Grace. But she went through it and forgave me and God delivered me and has blessed me in the Christian experience since that time.

Out of that experience I learned an important lesson. I had developed what I call a mental mirror. Whenever I sat in judgment of a brother Christian, or tried to pass judgment on anybody else, I put up my mental mirror and looked at myself, and then I could not judge anybody. God taught me that when He delivered me from that gambling.

CHRISTINE

This is 1989. I am four months short of being 80. I will have a real birth day in 1992 because there is a February 29 in that year. As for this year I will have to settle for March 1 as my birthday. I praise and thank God not only for this physical life, but I can praise God for the new life that he gave me in Christ Jesus.

I think Deanne was eighteen years old when she married Bruce Damschroder. Years later they moved out to Lakemoor in McHenry County where they attended the Alliance Bible Church.

We went out into the country to visit on week-ends and, on Sunday, went to the Alliance Bible Church to fellowship with the congregation there. I don't remember the year.

I remember that Christine attended high school in Chicago although I cannot think of the name of it offhand. I do not think where she attended high school is as important as the fact that she earned straight A's all the way to graduation.

She came home after school and I asked her, "Don't you have any homework to do, honey?"

No, she did not have any homework to do. I said, "How come? Other kids have homework to do."

"I do it in study periods," she told me.

How can a father complain when his daughter earns straight A's on a report card? She graduated at the age of sixteen. She went to a Christian college for one year. Then she was out for the summer and wanted to stay with Deanne out at Lakemoor for a while. Actually, I think she wanted to move out there. I suppose every teen-ager wants to break away from the home fires and get settled, personally, in their own lives or while they are making decisions.

There is one thing about Chris. She was a born-again girl practically from the start. At the age of four or five she accepted Christ and reiterated that later. During her teen-age years there were young people interested in the Youth for Christ meetings in most high schools. Ron Hutchcraft was the leader of Youth for Christ in the area. He is now the head of Youth for Christ in New York City and he is quite a well-known speaker on the radio. He is on Moody Bible Institute's WMBI radio station and every week he has a program for young people.

Chris, and some of her Christian friends, would choose a particular girl, and pray for her, and try to lead her to Jesus Christ, to show her how to ask Him to be her savior. There was a group of perhaps four or five girls, which grew into six or eight girls, and they began holding meetings. One time Ron Hutchcraft told them, "If you can get twenty-five kids here at our next meeting, I'll allow you to throw a pie in my face." I think there were forty kids or something like that at the next meeting. Those girls really went out and brought in a great group. They had loads of fun together.

During Christine's teen years Grace and I offered to drive kids all the way down to Moody Bible Institute in downtown Chicago, where once a month the Youth for Christ Clubs held a great central gathering. The auditorium seated thirty-five hundred people and that place would be loaded with teen-agers. We took a carload of people downtown every month and sometimes we had to borrow an extra car because so many wanted to go. We each drove a car full. We did not even have time for supper, so we dropped the kids off and went somewhere to eat, and then came back in time to catch the message. We heard Don Loney speak there a couple of times, a great youth man who spoke to kids and they listened. Many times there was a great outpouring of the Holy Spirit down at that place.

THE MOVE TO WONDER
LAKE AND RETIREMENT

Deanne called me up one day while we were living in Chicago on Irving Park Road. I answered the phone and heard, "Daddy, you have got to come out here to Lakemoor, to move out here."

I said, "What are you talking about?"

She said, "We need a Sunday school superintendent."

I said, "Honey, I am a Sunday School Superintendent at Mayfair."

"I know, but we need one, so we're praying for you to come out here."

A few days later she called me up and told me about a house that was for sale out there. She said Mom and I should come out and look at it. I have no idea why we went out there, but we did and the house was already sold. I said, "See, the Lord doesn't want me out here. Besides, I don't retire for six-and-a-half years yet."

"Well, we're going to pray you out here," she replied.

To make a long story short, we went out there another time looking at houses, and bought one in Wonder Lake, where I am sitting right now in the living room. We have been here twenty-one years. Grace moved out here on

September 15, 1970. I stayed in the house in Chicago with my mother during the week and we came out week-ends. Mother would not move out here until she had sold her house in the city which was completed on December 15 so we moved everything to the new house then.

We had turned an unheated porch into an enclosed, heated, area for a family room to provide more space. We gave my mother the second bedroom. She lived with us for ten years before she went home to be with the Lord. For several years we also had Grace's mother living with us.

When I moved out here I was still working in Chicago. So I drove back and forth from Wonder Lake to Chicago, three-and-a-half years, working nights, and it was a good time. And then I turned sixty-two.

Now, there were two men down at the barn arguing. They were both sixty-two years old. One wanted to retire at sixty-two, which meant he would receive 20% less in his monthly Social Security check than if he retired at full retirement age of sixty-five years. The other driver wanted to wait until he was sixty-five. There was a man, working at our depot, who was very good at calculating these things. He said, although the man who retired at sixty-two would collect 20% less income from Social Security, he would draw it for three years before the other man retired at sixty-five. The man who retired at sixty-five would receive his full Social Security income, but it would take him seven years to catch up to what the other man had already drawn in those three years between sixty-two and sixty-five. From then on he would be ahead of the other man as far as his Social Security income was concerned. I took all of this in and thought about it for a while.

I became sick about that time, and was down and out for three weeks. There was a policy in place that said if a driver was off work for more than two weeks, he could not work on a public conveyance unless he was cleared by our medical man. So I went downtown to be evaluated by the CTA's doctor. This was in March. I passed the medical check-up and went back to work.

I think the conversation between the two men who were contemplating retiring stuck with me. I thought, here I am, sixty-two years old, and I have been on the job for thirty-eight years. That gave me a hundred points in the calculation for my pension benefits. I needed ninety-two points to retire, so while I was downtown to see the doctor, I said to the man handling my case, "I want to see the retirement man."

He said, "Are you going to retire, Preacher?"

I said, "Well, I don't know, I may not, but . . ."

"Well, wait until you're going to retire," he said.

I said, "No, I want to go in and check these things out and I want to see my benefits counselor today."

"Okay," he said.

I went to the place he told me to go and met with the man in charge of retirement benefits. Earlier I had sat down and figured out, by the formula the CTA used to calculate pensions, what I thought I would get in pension income. I worked it out quite close to the exact amount. I was not sure of what I could get in Social Security income. I figured it would be about two hundred and forty dollars a month. I do not even remember what I received when I first retired.

Anyway, I went home and began thinking and planning. I was paying thirty-one dollars and nine cents per tank of gas, driving fifty-five miles into Chicago and fifty-five miles back every day, five days a week for a total of 550 miles per week. I was off Saturday and Sunday. I had enough seniority; I could pick my own run. I was getting six weeks' vacation at this time because I had over thirty-five years' service. So I sat down and figured out what I was spending and what I was earning.

For instance: I earned $533 for two weeks' work but when I got paid I had only $333 in my paycheck. So, $200 had been deducted for pension, Social Security, and all these other things. Then I calculated what my pension income would amount to, plus Social Security income, using the figures I had received downtown, to determine just how much money I would actually put in my pocket. I could earn a hundred-thousand dollars but if I put only ten dollars in my pocket every month, as far as I was concerned, I was making ten dollars. It took me three hours to come to the balance I was looking for.

Next I went in to talk to Grace where she was working on some beautiful needlework, and I said, "Honey, to the best of my ability, I have figured out that if I retire, my income will drop about in half but as far as the amount of money I put in my pocket each month is concerned, I will have $100 less. In other words, I am working, driving into Chicago for $25 a week extra.

She said, "Daddy, why don't you retire?"

I said, "I want you to know, though, I'm not going to retire making $6.69 an hour in Chicago and come out here and take a bus driving job for $2.95 an hour. If I retire, I retire."

"Fine" she said. "Retire."

I said, "Another thing. If I retire and take my full pension, it goes for the length of my life and then ceases. You will not receive any income when I die. However, I can take, I think it was two thirds, or a half, and your income would continue at that pace for you."

She said, "Retire, take your full pension, God will take care of me."

That was seventeen-and-a-half years ago and I have been retired ever since and blessed every minute of it.

CHURCH RESPONSIBILITIES AND FAMILY BLESSINGS

In January of 1971 we applied for membership at a church in McHenry, Illinois. We had made a pledge in Chicago that we would pay a certain amount of money toward the support of the church, and our missionaries, up to May. I did not want to renege on that pledge. So I went to the Chicago pastor and told him I would transfer my membership right away but that I would continue my giving to his church through May. Then I went to our new pastor in McHenry and told him what I was going to do and he said that was fine with him. And that is exactly what I did. At the end of May I transferred my giving to our new church.

God has blessed us down through the years. I am an Elder of the church in McHenry. I have been Sunday school superintendent here, worked in vacation Bible school, and been in charge of the balloon launches. These fun balloon launches, at the beginning of September, were used to invite folks to Sunday school. I went out visiting people to tell them about the Lord. I have participated in other various ministries also.

While I attended the church in Chicago we met for our regular Sunday morning service and then sometimes, in the afternoon, a bunch of us went out to a public park to hold another outdoor service. We put a loud speaker, which ran on a car battery, up in the fork of a tree, and Clem Bilhorn unfolded the organ that his grandfather had invented. It looked like a large suitcase when closed up but when he opened it, the case contained a pump organ. He pumped a bellows with his foot to produce the organ music and played it to accompany us in our singing of hymns and choruses. Soon we attracted interested and curious people and they stayed to hear Pastor Bartels preach a short message. Then we fanned out and passed out tracts and told folks about Jesus. People were born again at these meetings.

Once a month we went to the mental hospital with Clem. He took his pump organ and we did the same thing, singing for the patients. So we were busy.

We also went to a place in Chicago where criminals had been shooting at people out of windows, although not while we were there. We held open air meetings in the park at Cabrini Green. We set up a tarp in the middle of the field and started singing and the next thing we knew, kids came running out of those buildings, and we would have forty to fifty kids standing around listening to us. We talked to them and had certain types of Bible games to play and if they answered questions we gave them candy. After a while some of the parents came out to see what was going on. We preached the gospel there for years until it got too rough to go back. So, these were blessed times.

Grace and I have been church members in McHenry since 1971. We have been living here for twenty-one years. It has been a blessing all this time. God has been good. I am not as active as I once was. I am not a Sunday school superintendent, I do not teach a class, but I am a sort of a trouble shooter, in a sense, for our Pastor.

He has been with us for about six years. When he is completely swamped and cannot keep up with everything he is called upon to do, I may get a call from him, maybe on a Wednesday afternoon. He asks if I can lead Wednesday evening's prayer meeting and I agree to help out in that way. Or, when people are in the hospital, and Pastor does not have time to visit all of them, he asks me if I can help with that and so I do. For instance, just this last Friday I went to visit a man who used to be an Elder of the church, who had moved away. He was at Good Shepherd Hospital. So, I help Pastor out with things like that as much as I can and as he needs me.

Grace and I have had charge of the ministry at the nursing home in Woodstock, Illinois for some time now. There might be fifteen to twenty people come into the room where we are ministering. I lead our group in singing and then I tell people about Jesus and his salvation. Then we walk around and speak to the patients about what they have heard, and we pray with those who ask us to. Some pray to accept Jesus as their Savior.

I remember on two separate occasions that we went to the nursing home to minister to folks and nobody went with us. Not one volunteer was able to go with us. No piano player, no other singers. Grace and I stood up there gallantly singing out the songs by ourselves. I preached the gospel, and then we went around visiting with people until time to leave. We went back to church on Sunday and told everyone what a blessing that had been. We had all of the blessing to ourselves.

I went to this Woodstock nursing home today, November 10, 1991. Grace no longer goes. She thinks younger people should take this ministry. But recently a young lady has been coming with her family and others. I am so caught up with these people that I like to go. So I went today and brought at least ten other people with me to minister to these sick folks. We all sang, and then I brought a short message from the Bible. Then we mingled with the people and talked with them and gave them tracts and magazines that I save. It was a delightful blessing.

I do praise the Lord that I am not ashamed of the Gospel of Christ as it says in the Bible. God, right from the very beginning, placed His Holy Spirit in my heart. I love the Lord Jesus Christ. I have not always been faithful but God has been faithful, Jesus has been faithful, the Holy Spirit has been faithful in my life, bringing me under conviction when I am doing things wrong, causing me to see that wrong, and confess it before God. The Bible declares in I John 1:9 (KJV) "If we confess our sins He is faithful and just to forgive us our sins and to cleanse us from all unrighteousness." There are many times when I have to go to the Lord and ask for a renewing of my mind and heart. I ask Him to build up my faith, to take away the stress, and God is faithful. He has done it.

As you know, Grace and I have three daughters. We also have eight grandchildren and five great-grandchildren so far. My daughter said I should say what I would like to leave of myself to the world. Well, to God be the glory. He has saved people that I have talked to down through the years. He has used me as a vessel of honor. There are times when I am not feeling like a vessel of honor but God is faithful. He said, "My word will not return unto me void but shall accomplish that for which I sent it." (Isaiah 55:11 KJV) I believe God. I believe His promises. There are two things God cannot do. He cannot deny Himself and he cannot lie. If God promises in the Bible, His Word, that He is going to do something, or if He promises you something, He will do it. I believe it and that settles it.

Westminster Gospel Tract Reporting Company used to publish a calendar card printed on plastic. On it was written "God said it," with scripture under it, "Jesus did it," with scripture under it, "I believe it," with scripture under it, and "that settles it," with scripture under it. I bought a couple hundred of them and passed them all around. In fact, many years later I wrote to the company and asked them to renew that card and to send me a thousand more because it is true. God said it, Jesus did it, I believe it, and that settles it. Praise the Lord.

I have found, in my later years, that in a few instances, I have failed my children. Things have come back to me which prove that I was wrong in some minor instances. I have tried to set things straight. The hunger and desire of my heart is that my children will continue with Jesus for their entire lives. I believe they will.

My grandchildren have confessed Jesus Christ as Savior and Lord. There are needs in their lives as there are with all of us. So for my grandchildren and my great grandchildren, whom I love with all my heart, whether they are right or wrong in their actions, even if their lives are messed up, I love them. I will always embrace them to my bosom and help in whatever way I can. I think that God is faithful and I trust Him.

I have had regrets, very definite regrets, regarding Grace and the hardship and the hurts and the times when

I caused her deep distress. I know there were times when she thought of leaving me, but she hung around because of the two girls, Rae Ann and Deanne and stayed with me. She forgave me. There was love there but there was a certain amount of respect that must have been lost because of my actions. I regret that.

There have been times in my Christian experience when I have had doubts but God brought me through those doubts and renewed my mind and heart. There were times when I wondered, is it all worthwhile? Does it pay dividends, I mean, is it true?

There were doubts, however, the Spirit of God had planted that salvation in my heart and His Word declares, "He that hath begun a good work in you will perform it until the day of Jesus Christ. (Philippians 1:6 KJV) That is God's promise to me. There were times when I hung on by a thread to a promise like this in the Bible. It blessed my heart. It encouraged me. There are not enough cassette tapes in the world for me to put down the blessings that God has poured upon my life and upon my family.

I believe the blessings were planned by God before the foundation of the earth. I believe that he knew me before he made the earth. I believe that I was clear in His mind from ages past. I believe He brought me to salvation so that He could bless my life. I am sorry that I did not do it sooner but blessings, yes, I am full of blessings. I am full of gains. Do I have money? No. I have never had much money although I have always had enough.

I never made more than thirteen-thousand dollars a year in my entire life. That is what I was making when I retired and yet, I own my own home; it is a beautiful little place. We love it. It is great.

Even though we have had our storms, our problems, down through the years, God has blessed us as a family. He has watched over us. I believe there are angels assigned over us to keep us. I could tell story upon story where God has brought us through a problem.

For instance; I do not know anything about cars and when I buy a car I tell the Lord I know it is His car, I am just driving it. When the car breaks down I tell the Lord, "Lord, your car is sick. Would you please heal it?" Innumerable times God has brought somebody along right at that moment to help me and to get me through the situation and "healed" the car. Praise God from whom all blessings flow.

Have there been defeats? Yes, certainly, Satan has defeated me. My wicked heart has defeated me. My own mind has defeated me but through it all God has brought the victory.

Just recently I had a bronchial cough and was sick enough to call my doctor for an appointment but he was on vacation. I said to Grace "What in the world is going on here? The car has been broken down for two weeks, I cannot get to the doctor, my lovely wife is also sick, and other things are happening so what is God trying to tell me?"

Grace is stronger than I am and her cough was not as bad as mine. She said, "This too will pass."

And so these times of supposed defeats were sometimes necessary to set me aside and make me look inward and say, "Lord, why have you backed me up here? What is it I am to see? What is it you want to tell me?" Then I come to the end of self, which is where God wanted to bring me. He said, if he loves me he will chastise me, and he does. He will bring me up against the wall and I do not know where to go, up or down or sideways, and I will finally say, "Lord, I've come to the end of myself. Please forgive me, please help me." And that is exactly what the Lord is waiting for. He is waiting for me to get to the end of self and ask for help and then he comes in and he restores me.

Right this minute I am weeping because of feelings but they are blessed feelings of joy. They are feelings of thankfulness. We are getting near the day of Thanksgiving but I thank God every day.

I believe that we have a wonderful family situation. I think we all love one another a great deal. There have been differences of opinion down through the years, and perhaps even today. I do not know what my daughters, my grandchildren, or my great grandchildren think of me. I believe they love me. I believe they think well of me but I do not recall any of them ever coming up to me and telling me any incident in life that was special to them or anything like that. I suppose they have some. I have many. I thank the Lord that most of my family is in agreement on the very essence of life and that is Jesus Christ, Savior, Lord of Glory, King of Kings and coming again. I believe that this is the foundation of our family.

I read The Chicago Tribune every day and my heart fails me. From what I read, it seems to me, as the Bible teaches, that we are in the last days of our world as we know it. The Bible says that society will become as it was in the days of Noah when God determined there were only eight people left who believed in Him. Every day there is some story about how people demean Christian principles. Even in America, where we have freedom of religion, Satan's forces of evil are gathering. I believe hard times are coming for Christians. I do not know that I will be around here, being at my age, but I pray that God will surround my family with His angels during hard times to come. I pray they will stand strong in the truth, strong in Jesus, and never deny him even through suffering and persecution. I think there are powerful leaders within my family and the Christian faith. I am not mentioning names. I love each and every one of them and trust Jesus will keep each one in his hands.

MORE STREETCAR STORIES FROM 1936 TO 1946

I have told a little bit about some of the men I worked with during the ten years I was a streetcar conductor. I also had some other experiences I would like to tell about. For instance, one night around nine o'clock, my motorman and I, working our streetcar, were heading north on Western Avenue, down near Archer Avenue and three young males got on. They were quite young, maybe seventeen or eighteen. They had been drinking. One of them was so drunk he had to be helped up onto the platform of the streetcar. However, they were actually no problem. They paid their fare, and went inside the sliding door on my right, and sat on the long seat facing the center aisle of the car.

My motorman drove another short distance to our next stop where another young man was waiting to get on the streetcar. He was also inebriated. He got on and paid his ten-cent fare. He stood at the end of the platform, near the edge of it, and I was quite concerned about him. It is an open ended car and it was going along, at full speed, perhaps thirty-five miles an hour. It could run at forty-five miles an hour if it has had a long run or is on a downhill slope. Although my passenger was tipsy he seemed to be holding his balance. He was carrying a little folded bag which looked as if it might contain a sandwich and he had this little smile on his face. I said to him, "How you doin' tonight?"

He smiled at me. He said, "I'm doin' fine."

I said, "Great. Would you like to go in and sit down, it's getting a little chilly out here."

"Yeah, I'm going to go in and sit down," he said.

I opened the door and he went in. He could not have been in there longer than five minutes when there was a storm and a commotion. Oh my goodness. I opened the door to find the first three drunks sitting on the side seat and above them somebody had smashed eggs, and, of course, the eggs had splattered down on them. They were a mess. One of them was standing up and yelling for blood. I bellowed, "What has happened to my streetcar?"

"That guy threw eggs at us," and he pointed to the young fellow who had the little sandwich bag. He was sitting quietly in the center of the streetcar. I walked over to him and leaned over him and I said as calmly as I could, "Sir, could I have a word with you out on the platform, please?"

"Oh, sure," he said.

I walked back out onto the platform. He came to the door and opened it and he said, "Are you going to call the police?"

I had a difficult time trying to keep from laughing. I put a stern look on my face and said, "No, son, I don't feel it's necessary to call the police but I certainly have a problem here."

"Yeah," he said, "I suppose you do but it sure was fun." He said, "If you want, I'll get off."

I said, "Well. . ." but he went back inside and sat down. I followed him inside to be sure there were no more ruckuses.

In the meantime, two of the other three guys held their buddy back to keep him from storming the egg cracker. I said to the angry man, "Come out on the platform and cool off for a minute." He came out and stomped around while I went back inside to the two fellows who were not quite so drunk.

One of them said, "We're going to take that guy. We're going to beat up on him."

I said, "Do you know who that is?" You know, I was not a Christian in those days. Lying came easy. Stories came easy. So I said, "He is the champion boxer of the Navy Yard in north Chicago." I said, "He would wipe up the floor with you three guys. My suggestion to you guys is to hold your buddy down and just let it ride!"

"We traveled a few more blocks and the egg throwing fellow said, "I'll get off here."

I said, "Thank you," and he got off. The situation developed, it calmed down, and eventually my motorman and I got through the night. That was one little event that happened and I laughed about it for a long time. I have never forgotten that story.

There was another occurrence. I told previously that I worked with Old Diamond Johnny on Division Street on the night bus. Later on, I got another motorman who later became a superintendent, and still later in his life he shot himself to death. I cannot remember his name. We worked together, he as the motorman and me as the conductor. We were making a trip on Division Street, going east. We were late and could not make up the time. This motorman, I will call him Al, said to me, "We can cross over at Halsted Street. Instead of going as far east as Wells Street, we'll go only to Halsted Street. We can take the crossover on Halsted and come back." That is a shortcut of six blocks each direction.

I said, "There's no crossover at Halsted Street."

"I know how to do it," he said.

I said, "Are you sure?"

"I'm sure. When we get to Halsted we back up over onto the Halsted Street line going north, then come forward again and around onto the west bound track on Division."

"Oh," I said. "By the time we do all that we could go down the mile to Wells Street and come back . . ."

"No," he said, "We can do it. I know how to do it."

I, as the conductor, was the boss. "Okay," I said. "We'll try it."

We got down to Division and Halsted and my motorman backed up onto Halsted, and then drove forward turning the corner back from Halsted to Division Street west, and as he did so, the front trucks of our streetcar derailed. That is a set of four large steel wheels that run on the streetcar track. They dragged the car down to the curb. Well! My heart dropped. We are fired, I thought. We are done. We have had it.

In the meantime a northbound Halsted Street streetcar drove up and the motorman got off and came over to take a good look at our disaster. He asked, "What in the world happened?"

"We're in trouble," I said. "We've derailed. I'll have to go find a phone and call in to get the wreck wagon out here to put the trucks back on the rails, and here we are on the wrong street. We are going to get fired!"

"Wait a minute," he said, "I think we can help. We have a drawbar on our car." He got the drawbar and he and his conductor hooked one end of it onto the front end of his streetcar and the other end to the back end of our streetcar. They had some kind of iron bars and one man guided the wheels with the bars while the motorman of the other car pulled our car backwards. They were able to pull that set of wheels back onto the streetcar rails. My motorman drove our car around the corner back on to Division Street and we were ready to go back west. We thanked these men and one of them said, "I won't report it, and we'll just keep it quiet."

"Thanks," I said.

By this time, instead of making up the time, we were half an hour later than we were before. When we got back to the other end of our run, and started back east again, the boss came out of the barn and said, "People have been complaining. Where have you guys been?"

"Oh," I said, "We were a little bit late and things happened and we just got mixed up which made us a little bit later but we'll be back on time on the next trip." We could run fast and make up the time. We had a certain amount of running time and if there was little traffic on Division Street we could pick up the speed.

I think I ought to mention this. When we finished two trips to 200 west at Wells Street, on the next trip we went only to 1600 west which was near Milwaukee Avenue and Ashland Street. When we got to Milwaukee and Ashland, there was a crossover where we could reverse from east bound to west bound. When we got there we changed ends of the streetcar by switching the motorman's station to the conductor's platform and the conductor's platform to the motorman's station. Then we waited for the Milwaukee Avenue streetcar to arrive before we started back west.

There were ladies who worked downtown in the office buildings. They worked until two o'clock in the morning. They came north on the Milwaukee line and half-a-dozen of them usually got off of or onto our streetcar and rode west, some of them all the way to California Avenue. I mean no disrespect, but most of these ladies were Polish, and they spoke animatedly and loudly. They all seemed to love me. They smiled at this pretty, handsome, streetcar conductor and they made playful remarks to one another. I teased them a bit although I did not know any Polish. I winked at them when they got off, and said good night, and I used to love to have the Polish ladies get on my bus.

As you know, I was not a Christian during these ten years on the streetcars. I was one of the boys. I was a somewhat well-liked fellow, a nice guy and I was friendly with many of the men I worked with. There was a small group of us who went out together a lot. We went to the race track and we played poker together. We enjoyed one another.

A number of the men and their wives joined Grace and me every third Saturday. We had what we called an outing of the CTA men. When we went on these outings we each put in a dollar into the pot to buy a bottle of whiskey. I would drink a high-ball, and then I might have a second one, but I sipped it because, if I drank more than two, I became sick and I did not like that much. Some of the men drank that bottle down within an hour and they would go out to buy a second bottle. I never chipped in on the second bottle. I did not want any more whiskey. One of the men often got stoned during the night's fun and went home blind drunk. I felt sorry for him, but that was the way he was. Others became moderately drunk. I used to dance with the other men's wives, as they danced with Grace. It was an excuse to quit drinking after a couple of drinks. It was a part of the partying and nothing dirty about it, nothing suggestive. I do not believe there was ever any propositioning. I never propositioned any of the other wives. I did not dance a lot because my desire was the gambling. Playing poker, shooting craps, that is what I had a yen for and what I did more than anything else.

I first started on the job in January, 1936. That February was extremely cold. I think the temperature was below zero, such as 10, 12, or 15 degrees below zero, every day for the entire thirty days. We conductors worked on outside open platforms of the streetcar. Some of the men's thumbs froze as they worked their changers making change for passengers. These were made of metal and they held quarters, dimes, and nickels, so that we could push a plunger on the quarter slot, for instance, and a quarter would drop out for us to give change to the passenger. Some of the men's toes froze also. I was not supposed to step inside the car to collect money, or to use the bell cord, which I pulled two times to tell the motorman to go ahead, or once to tell him to stop at the next corner. If there was trouble in the rear, and I needed help, I pulled the cord three times to stop for an emergency.

I had spent my last three-and-a-half or four dollars for a pair of boots that came all the way up the calves, extra-large. I filled the inside bottoms with newspaper, wore two pairs of heavy socks, and my cap, and worked with gloves on with the fingers cut off. When I came into the barn one day the assistant boss came up to me and said, "Chris, where's your ear muffs?"

I said, "I don't have any ear muffs."

He took his off his ears and put them on mine. He said, "You take these. I'll get another pair." Some of the men had to have their thumbs and toes split to heal them because they had become frozen. My fingers and toes did not freeze but I broke the rules in order not to freeze. I worked inside the streetcar.

One other incident happened on the streetcars. I was working with a motorman whose name I do not remember. There was a short break up at Roscoe Street right behind Lane Technical High School on Western and Addison. Roscoe was two blocks before Addison traveling north. There was a turn-around there and the company scheduled extra busses in there to haul high school kids south when school let out. It was a turn-around that we used sometimes when we made a trip down to 111th or 79th to the south and then came back north. Instead of going all the way up to Howard, we went only to Roscoe, into the turn-around, and back south to Division Street. We could pull into the depot for the end of our run from there.

Well, there again, the streetcar conductor had to hold up the lever that opened the switch in the rails that allowed the streetcar into this turn-around. It was a winter day terribly icy. I got out and lifted up the lever to switch the rails. As the car passed me I was supposed to let go of the lever, grab a bar at the back end of the car, and jump up onto the platform. I was to give the motorman a signal by pulling the bell cord to tell him I was on the car and he could go.

This day I lifted the lever, and because the road was icy and slippery, when the back end came around to me, I missed it and did not get on the streetcar. My motorman went around the circle, back out into the street, and started south toward Belmont Avenue. I was not on the streetcar! I ran behind it hollering, "Hey, hey, wait for me," but he did not hear me. He got to Belmont Avenue, two blocks down, where he caught the red light. I ran as fast as I could to catch up to him. I must have been a funny sight. I thought he would wait until he heard the two-ring, go ahead signal from me when the light turned green. But, the light turned green, he took off, there he went, and I was still running.

The only chance I had to catch up with my car was to ride the streetcar behind it. My motorman made a number of stops because of street lights, or traffic, but kept going without any signals from me. How could he be unaware that I was not on the streetcar? We were traveling south to Division Street, which was usually quite busy, so it was amazing that no passengers wanted to get on or off for that whole distance. My motorman finally had to stop for a traffic light at Division. I saw him come to the back of our streetcar, and look around for me, but I was still a block away on the car behind him. He sat there until the car I was on pulled up behind him. I scrambled off of it and onto my own streetcar and he said, "Where have you been?"

I could have punched him one but I said, "I didn't get on the platform back at Roscoe Street. You did not hear any go-ahead bells from me so why did you keep going? You came all the way to Division alone."

"I didn't," he exclaimed.

"You did!" I said.

"I didn't!" he said.

"You absolutely did," I said, "but we won't tell anybody." I went over and lifted up the switch, went around the corner, got on the back end of the platform and we went into the depot, through with the day's work.

At the time, the incident was a bit frustrating; however, I can laugh about it now. I wonder what I looked like running down the street in my uniform, screaming for the streetcar to wait for me. I am glad no one had a camera handy.

BUS DRIVING EXPERIENCES

I am going to relate a couple of bus driving stories. These experiences that come to me are not necessarily in chronological order. I may tell you something that comes to mind that happened on my bus in 1965 and in the telling of it I may remember a story that happened back in 1945 on the streetcars. I will identify it as either a streetcar or a bus experience and if possible I will give an approximate time if I know it.

On the busses, in my early bus driving days, I drove on Western Avenue. It was an extremely wide street at this point. Clybourn Avenue came up diagonally from the south and ended at Belmont and Western. Traffic came off of Clybourn Avenue and merged onto Western.

One time I had driven into the Roscoe turn-around and all of my passengers had disembarked. That was as far as I was to go before heading back south to the depot. It was a winter day and the streets were icy. I left Roscoe and headed south to Belmont Avenue, two blocks away, which was usually heavy with traffic. About a block down the street my bus began to fishtail. I lost complete control of it. There was one man riding with me at the time. The bus turned completely around, crossed over to the other side of the street, and came to rest at the curb at the bus stop on the first street north of Belmont Avenue, just before the busy intersection where Clybourn merged into Western and Belmont. It was facing in the opposite direction for the side of the street where it halted. Amazingly, with all the traffic that went through that section, not a single car or streetcar came north. My lone passenger said, "Wow. That was something." An understatement if I ever heard one.

I tried to reply calmly and said, "Yes, it sure was."

I do not believe I was a Christian at that point. I do not remember how far back that went.

Another time, I was driving on Milwaukee Avenue. Again, I do not remember whether I was a Christian or not. This was in the fall and a cold rain was pouring down. It was not snowy or icy but it was slippery. The streets were made of bricks at that time, imbedded with streetcar rail, and a lot of grease and oil had collected on them since the last rain.

I was heading north when my brakes locked and I began to skid. I had reduced my speed to about one mile an hour, however, the bus kept skidding. Because the tracks and bricks were elevated a bit higher, and the street sloped down to the curb on the side, and it was icy, my bus just kept going one mile an hour. There was no way I could stop it. There were steel posts along the curb and it slid into one of the posts with the front left corner of the bus. The impact knocked me out of my seat and onto my back. It tore the shoe off of my left foot and damaged my big toe. My shoe was caught between the brake and the base of the driver's seat.

I was lying on my back on the floor when the emergency people came and took me to the hospital. The steering wheel had hit me in the left thigh and I had a hematoma. That was blood that had accumulated on the inside of the injury. The doctor said he did not want the outside of the injury to heal with that loose blood in there. So he took about a yard of gauze, stuck it inside the hole in my leg, and bandaged it. I went back to see him a couple of days later and he pulled out the soaked gauze and inserted a shorter piece. After another couple of days, I went back, and he pulled that out. He said that way, the healing begins on the inside of the leg, and it does not keep the blood from seeping out. Otherwise it would have healed on the outside and all that blood would have been contained on the inside. It would have had to be cut and drained later anyway. This way, the doctor kept putting shorter pieces of gauze in there until it healed, from the inside out. I think I was off work for a week or ten days until it healed up. All he did with my toe was to bind the big one to the next toe because it was not broken, only sprained.

Here is another story. I believe this is the first person I led to Jesus Christ as a bus driver. I came out of the loop on the Milwaukee Avenue night bus and picked up a man who was nicely drunk. He was not ferocious, he was happy, and he began whistling gospel songs and tunes. I looked back at him and said, "Hey, fella." He came up to the front seat that ran sideways right inside the door. I said, "I bet I can tell you where you learned those songs."

He said, "Yeah, where?"

I said, "In one of the mission ministries downtown or in church."

"No, I learned them in jail." He grinned.

"Oh," I said. "Great. Do you know what you're whistling?"

"Yeah," he replied.

I said, "Do you know the Lord Jesus as your savior?"

"Oh," he said. "I love Jesus."

I said, "That's wonderful." I said, "But do you know him as your personal savior?"

"Oh, I love Jesus," he said again.

We arrived at the end of the line and I moved from the driver's seat to sit next to Patty on that long bench seat. I had my Bible out and I said, "Patty, I'm going to ask you one more time. Have you accepted Jesus as your personal savior from sin?"

He said, "I love Jesus."

I said, "You're not answering my question." I had about eight minutes lay-over time at the north end there. However, I sat with Patty about six minutes past my leaving time. In that fourteen minutes he did not pray to confess his sins and to receive Jesus into his heart although he kept saying he loved Jesus. I showed him the plan of salvation from verses in my Bible. Finally I said, "Patty, I'm already late leaving the end of the line. I can't spend any more time with you. I'm going to take off. It's time for me to go." By then I was already six minutes late. We were supposed to be fifteen minutes apart on the all-night busses at that time.

I started off down the street. I had not gone two blocks when Patty hollered out, "I wanna accept Jesus as my Savior." He was the only one on the bus so I pulled over to the curb and parked. I got out of my driver's seat and sat down next to Patty once again. I prayed with him to receive Jesus Christ as his Savior and Lord of his life. When we finished praying he thanked me.

In the meantime, the driver who was supposed to be fifteen minutes behind me, had gone around me, and had headed for the loop. I said, "Patty, I'm amiss on my job. I gotta get going."

We had a lot of running time on that run, so it was easy for me to make up time, if I kept going. The driver ahead of me was doing all the work until I caught up to him, a few blocks before the loop, and passed him. When I came back out of the loop I had picked up enough time, and was on time where I belonged.

Three weeks later, I was driving down Milwaukee Avenue through Logan Square, and once again it was raining. I looked out the window and across the street I saw Patty walking along, drunk. I stopped my bus. I opened the window and hollered, "Patty Keller. You get over here right away." He came running across the street and got on my bus. I gave him the fare. I said, "Put the fare in the fare box," which he did. I said, "Patty, just two weeks ago you accepted Christ as your Savior and changed your life, and here I find you a few weeks later, drunk. Your life hasn't changed a bit."

He looked at me with his sad eyes and said, "Charlie, what did you expect? I've been drinking for thirty-five years. Did you expect me to stop right now?" And you know, I learned from this experience not to judge another man. God was impressing on me, Patty is in my hands now and I will deal with him and his problems. You pray that he may continue walking with me. I saw Patty one or two times after that but then he was out of my life and I expect to see Patty in heaven. He was born-again. He accepted Christ, loves Jesus. I do not know what happened in his life later on. So that was Patty. That was the first experience I had in leading someone to Jesus on the bus.

Western-Berwyn Terminal 1959

As a night shift bus driver I went to work at twenty minutes to nine at night and then I was finished at twenty minutes to six in the morning. One time, probably in the 1960s, I came out of the loop carrying enough passengers to comprise a small group of seated people. When I came to Clark Street at Division Street a black man, who looked to be middle aged, boarded the bus. He had been drinking but he did not make a fuss. He paid his fare and went back and sat down in the middle of the bus. I continued delivering people home. He dozed off. When I arrived up north, near the end of my run, near Howard Street, I had only two little old ladies left on the bus besides this man. The ladies got off a couple of blocks apart, and then this fellow woke up and came to the front of the bus near my driver's seat. "Where's I at?" he said.

I said, "You're right near the city limits on the north side," I said, "Where do you want to go, where do you want to get off?"

He looked at me and said, "Well," he said, "Maybe I's gonna hold you up."

"Oh, man," I said, "That's a bad thought." I said, "Do you know, if you hold up a bus driver while he's in the process of driving a bus, you get a year in jail and a ten thousand dollar fine?"

He pulled out a knife and opened it up and said, "Well," he said "Maybe I's gonna hold you up."

To be perfectly honest, I was frightened. I looked out, looked to see if there was some kind of patrol car going by. I was ready to flash my lights or do something but I had to bear up. There was nobody in sight. I said, "Man, you're making a big mistake." Now let me pause here.

I am convinced that God gave me a certain amount of discernment where I could line up a situation, make a decision on how to approach it, one way or another, and step right into it. When this man took out his knife, I said, "Boy, that's a big mistake, it ain't gonna work, and you're gonna be in deep trouble." In the meantime, I reached down into my bag and pulled out my little pen knife that I sharpen pencils with, and opened it up. I flung it full force into the wooden tray next to my register. It stuck there and quivered! Then I reached out and pulled it out of there, holding it in my hand and I said, "You know, fella, when I was in the Marines, they taught me how to cut a man's heart out and throw it in his face before he died" and I just glared at him as mean as I could look.

He said, "Do you know how to use that knife?" He looked at me with a surprised look on his face and said, "Yessir, I believes ya." He closed up his knife and put it back in his pocket. I took a deep sigh down to my toes. A couple of blocks later he said, "I'll get off here," and he stumbled down the steps and off my bus. When I went south again I looked for him because I was not going to pick him up again.

Telephones had been installed in the busses in the last years that I worked, although I did not use them much. Sometimes I made a pretense of using one by holding the button down to scare off some people that might be threatening me, but I seldom used it unless there was actually an emergency. This time I called the dispatcher to report this incident.

Another experience was when I pulled into the Howard Street turn-around one night, around one-thirty, for my half hour lunch break or fallback. I usually went over to the restaurant for a hard roll with jelly and coffee, or if I was really hungry, I bought a sandwich, and then I returned to the bus. This night I sat and relaxed, with the lights off, until it was within about eight minutes of my leaving time. I pulled up to where I began my run and opened the doors to the bus. I sat there reading my New Testament, when all of a sudden, a young man jumped up the steps and into the bus. He had a jacket over one arm and an open knife in his other hand. He said, "Okay, Grandpa, we get goin' right now."

I stopped reading and looked at him and said, "Well, son, I can't leave yet. I have to wait until its one fifty before I leave here."

"We go right now, grandpa!" he said, "They're after me."

I said, "Oh? Who's after you?"

89

"Those black guys out in the tavern." This young man, I found out later, was an East Indian. He looked to be between eighteen and twenty years of age, in that area, and he was apparently frightened that these men were after him. Again he said, "We go!"

I explained to him, "Son, I don't dare leave now, you see, you don't understand. The night busses have to make connections with other busses because people are going to work, and if I leave now, I'll be too early. Maybe people who need to make a connection will miss it. They have to catch my bus." I tried to quiet him down while talking calmly. I said, "Why don't we just talk about this for a minute." My bus was in neutral with the emergency brake on. I climbed off the bus and he followed me.

Just as I did so, two policemen, with three or four people behind them, appeared from around the bend that leads to the elevated streetcar entrance, across the street. The policemen came upon the young man with their guns drawn. He turned from me and began to back off, waving the knife back and forth in one hand, and carrying his jacket in the other. He shouted, "Stay away from me! Stay away from me!"

The policemen aimed their guns at him with both hands, and they kept shouting back, "Drop the knife! Drop the knife!"

Here, again, the discernment of the Lord came upon me. This boy did not have, what I call, a switch-blade knife, and that registered with me. He had a large pen knife. As the police began to approach him, demanding he drop the knife, the boy continued to back up and wave his knife around. "Wait a minute." I said, "Let me talk to him," and I started to walk toward him. I did not want the police to shoot him. I looked at the young man and said "Son, I'm sure you don't want to stab anybody."

"No, but they're after me." His whole body was shaking.

I said, "Well listen. I don't want these policemen to shoot you, either. This is silly." I said, "Why don't you put the knife down and we'll talk things over. Let the policemen come over here and we'll talk. I want you to know I'm your friend." He looked around wildly for a moment or two and finally threw the knife down. The policemen were on him immediately. They got him down on the ground and handcuffed his hands behind his back. I kneeled down beside him and he looked up at me with these dark brown eyes and said, "You deceived me."

I smiled at him and said, "No, son, I did not deceive you. I told you I didn't want the police to shoot you and I didn't want you to hurt someone and be in deep trouble. I want you to know I am your friend."

While all of this was happening the bus driver behind me came up into the place where he was to have his fallback. He saw the commotion and came over to me and said, "Preacher, what's going on here?"

I said, "I'll tell you later. Help me get this young man up on his feet." The policemen had not helped me get him up. This driver and I helped him stand. As I talked to him I put a gospel track in his pocket. He said he did not want that religious stuff and I told him "Well, you're going to go down to the police station for a while, you're going to sit for a long time, so why don't you take it and read it." In the meantime, I was about ten minutes late leaving because of all this tumult. The policemen took the man away and I jumped in my bus and took off. At least we did not have any blood shed for the bus to run over that particular night.

About two weeks later the man got on my bus again. He did not recognize me but I recognized him. I began talking to him and that is when I learned he was East Indian. He was quite against white people and their treatment of Indians. He was a bitter fellow who had no use for us. I tried to steer his thoughts to spiritual things but he did not respond very well.

Western-Berwyn Terminal around 1947-48

There was another experience I had during my fallback at that Howard Street turn-around. I think this was in the mid-1950s. I was out of fellowship with my Lord because of sin in my life, the sin of gambling. I was miserable. I was not reading my Bible. I was completely distressed in my heart, in my mind, and of all men most miserable as Pastor, and the apostle, Saint Peter put it. I was exhausted physically, emotionally, spiritually, however, I was still working and I continued to witness. I had gospel tracts on the bus, which I gave out to people, but my heart was not in it.

All I wanted to do was get up to Howard Street, pull into the back side of the turn-around, and park my bus. I wanted to lay down on the long seat and go to sleep. I drove the bus in there, parked, and turned out the lights. I went over to lie down on the long seat and I did not even get my back flat on the seat when there was a knock on the door. I grunted and groaned and got up and went to the door. A young man was out there, holding a sport jacket over his arm, and knocking on the door. I opened the door said, "Son, I'm on my fallback. I'm beat and I'm trying to get some rest."

He said, "Sir, I'm sorry to bother you, sir, but I wonder, I have a real good sport jacket here. Would you buy it from me for a dollar?"

He held the nice looking sport jacket up to show me. I said, "Son, I'm not interested in your sport jacket and I'm sorry but I need my rest."

He said, "Okay, I'm sorry sir. I'm sorry I bothered you," and he turned to walk away.

I went to lie down on my back and, if you are a Christian you will understand this, the Lord "said," although the Lord does not speak vocally, *Charles, what are you doing?* I said aloud, "Lord, leave me alone, I don't want to be bothered, I'm tired, I'm exhausted, don't bother me." *Charlie, you know what you did was not right.* "Yeah, I know." *Well do you not think you ought to do something about it?* "All right, Lord, get off my back." So I got up, turned on the lights, pulled my bus up to the entrance of the turn-around, and opened the door. The man was walking about half a block further north on Clark Street. Mind you, it is one-thirty to one-forty in the morning. I yelled, "Hey, son." He heard me and turned around and I motioned with my arm, come on back here. It took him a few minutes to get back to me and when he approached I said, "Man, I need to ask you to forgive me. I am a Christian. I didn't treat you right. I'm out of fellowship with my Lord and I'm miserable," and I said, "I mistreated you and I want to ask you to forgive me."

He said, "It's all right. It's okay, there's nothing to forgive."

I said, "Fine. Now let's start again right at the beginning. What was it you wanted?"

He said, "I wanted to know if you would buy my jacket because I haven't had anything to eat in a couple of days and I'm hungry."

I said, "We can remedy that." Now you could get a good meal for a dollar, at least you could get a hamburger with some French fries and a cup of coffee for about a dollar down at the little hamburger hut that was open all night. It was just a long block down at Clark and Devon. So I gave the boy a dollar. I said, "Why don't you go over to that restaurant and get yourself a hamburger or something," and I pointed him in the right direction.

He said, "Oh, great. Thank you," and he took off. I watched until he went into the hamburger hut. The time came for me to leave.

Two days later, at the same time, this young man came to my bus up at the turn-around and once again knocked at the door. I opened it and let him in and as he jumped up the steps into the bus he said, "You're my good luck piece." Oh, by the way, I had given him gospel tracts when I gave him the dollar and told him to read them. He said, "You're my good luck piece. You gave me that dollar so I went down to the hamburger place and not only did I get something to eat, but I got a job. It ain't much of a job, I'm only washing dishes in a hotel down there, but I get a room and I'm washing dishes and I've at least got something going." Then he said, "I got on to give you your dollar back."

I said, "Son, I don't want you to give me the dollar back. What I want you to do is, keep that dollar, and if you come across somebody who is in the same shoes you were in, give him the dollar, with the same instructions I'm giving you. Perhaps, when I get to heaven, that dollar may have become a million dollar blessing." He laughed and said okay he would do that. Of course, I talked about the Lord; I gave testimony of the Lord's goodness and salvation. He listened and thanked me and finally took off. That is the last time I saw this boy.

The hardest and most emotional experience I ever had on my bus was in 1968 during the Democratic National Convention in Chicago. There were thousands of activists downtown protesting the Viet Nam war. They were demonstrating against it. At the same time, about four hundred of our CTA bus drivers, of about three thousand drivers, had gone on a wildcat strike and were marching around some of our depots.

The strikers wanted better representation in the union and they were organizing violent confrontations in Lincoln Park. They smashed windows downtown, and there were a great many of Mayor Daley's police officers out, trying to keep the peace. They broke up rallies, and threw tear gas, and it was a fantastic, horrible night. I wrote a story called *The Blind Bus Driver* which follows, so I am not going to go into a lot of details here, but my opinion at the time was, just do your job. You pick people up, you let them off the bus at their stops, and you do not get involved in arguments. Try to keep things as peaceful as possible. Go about your work and you will be okay. The rest of the story is in the manuscript to follow.

For almost a week, there was a great contention on the street. At the beginning of the rioting none of us bus drivers would attempt to complete our runs below Fullerton Avenue. We would not go south as far as Lincoln Park because that is where the violence was taking place. The drivers got together and went to the boss and told him their fears and how they planned to restrict their runs to north of Lincoln Park. That meant not going into the loop. The boss understood our fears.

The second night out, after this restriction, I told the other drivers that was enough of that. I was going to do my job and drive down into the loop where I belonged. Most of the others did that too. It was quite a night.

Following is the story referenced above as it was sent in to periodical publishers.

THE BLIND BUS DRIVER

By

Charles M. Christensen

The date was August 28, 1968, the night of the Democratic National Convention in Chicago. The air was charged with tension. Every anti-war demonstrator and left-winger in the world came to converge on Chicago this night. Plus, in Charlie's own bus drivers' union, of the Chicago Transit Authority, there were about four-hundred of the three-thousand drivers calling for a wildcat strike. Charlie had never, in his more than thirty years of driving, seen so much agitation in the city. He was angry too, but for a different reason.

The drivers were standing around the table in the depot, writing out their trip sheets for their runs for the night. The talk was loud and boisterous with many drivers telling how they would handle any rowdies that got on their busses that night. Some drivers even carried guns, which of course, was against all rules.

After listening to the wild talk for some time Charlie finally spoke up. "You guys make me sick," he said. "You're getting paid to pick up passengers, collect fares, and make your runs. You're not supposed to judge people's politics, motives, or try to police the city. Just do your job and no one's going to bother you. Mind your own business and don't get involved."

He did not wait for any arguments. He took his trip sheet and his bus bag and headed for the parking lot to pick up his bus. He was not going to let himself get stirred up over this business. He thought, just drive your bus, be pleasant to everyone, and everything will be all right.

He noticed how quiet it was on the first trip south from Howard Street to the Chicago loop. No one spoke much. The Viet Nam war was the center of all the commotion along with the Democratic National Convention. To take sides, either way, about the war would just bring trouble on the bus, so he was grateful for the quietness.

Passing the Lincoln Park area he noticed how people were lining up along the curbs. Men were shouting anti-war slogans into loud speakers and generally fanning the flames of discontent.

On the way back north again the demonstrators were throwing stones and rocks at everything moving. None of the rocks hit the windows of his bus and he was thankful for that. He thought this is just kids having fun; there is no need to get upset.

On the second trip south toward the loop at eleven-forty, Charlie noticed that few people were riding. Again, as he passed Lincoln Park, most of the activity centered deeper into the park. As he approached Goethe Street he had four men and one lady on the bus. She wanted to get off. As he braked for the stop, he noticed a solid stream of people, forty abreast, coming to the corner. They were lined solidly, all the way back to the next corner west, and as he let the lady off, and before he could get started again, one man carrying a microphone yelled, "Get the bus!" The crowd surrounded the bus, then leaped up on the front bumper, tore the windshield wipers right off their mountings, and began to pound them into the windshield trying to break through.

They ripped off the rear view mirrors outside the bus on both corners and smashed windows. The windows splintered but did not literally break through. In one instance someone threw a brick squarely into the window. The passenger sitting there had just left his seat. Charlie was glad he had had the sense to warn the passengers to keep the windows closed that night. The three men sitting close to that smashed window, and other passengers, came forward cursing and yelling to Charlie to "run the XXX down."

Charlie glared at the five men on the bumper trying to smash the windshield. There was hate in their faces even though they had never seen him before. Even so, he knew he could not run them down. This was contrary to his training as a bus driver. He lifted his foot from the brake. As the bus began to move forward slowly, picking up speed, the men jumped, one by one, off the front bumper.

Finally, only one man was in the way. He stood in the street about twenty-five feet away in front of the bus with a megaphone to his mouth and he was shouting to the crowd. Charlie aimed his bus right at the man and gave it some gas. He watched as the man jumped to the curb. Charlie knew these "hard-core" commies were not about to sacrifice their lives for the cause. These instigators would let the suckers that they whipped into a frenzy do that. These men always disappeared when the confrontation got too hot.

Charlie drove his wounded bus out of the milieu and headed for Division Street. He prevented three other Broadway and Clark Street busses from heading into the same place he had just come from by stopping them, and rerouting them, and then he began to finish his trip. He felt obligated to take his passengers to the loop. These men were going to work on the night shift. It was difficult driving without mirrors but he was careful.

After dropping his last passenger off the bus, who by the way, cursed and ranted all the way downtown about the communists trying to overtake and ruin our country, Charlie stopped at a gasoline station to call his dispatcher. He gave him a report on what had happened. The dispatcher calmly said, "Okay, take your bus back to limits depot and pick up another bus."

Charlie remembered that when he had gone past the depot, there were four hundred or more dissident bus drivers marching around the depot, picketing. He mentioned this to the dispatcher. "I'll call the station and have the police take you through the picket lines," he said. When he arrived the police were ready. They broke through the picket lines and guided Charlie slowly to the depot. The pickets called Charlie "scab" and cursed him and he opened the window and yelled back, "at least I'm not a communist." He was stirred up and angry but trying to retain some semblance of control. After all, he had a bus to drive. The police led him out the back way, and he got into place at Halsted Street and Clark Street and headed back south.

It was now almost 2:00 a.m. No one was riding. As he reached Lincoln Park on his third trip people were streaming across Clark Street. Then he saw the reason why. There was a large cloud of some kind of white substance, which looked like smoke, following them. He figured it was tear gas. He was in the midst of the crowd within seconds and found himself unable to proceed because of the mass of people surrounding his bus. Then it began all over again.

They swarmed all around the bus and smashed windows and doors and threw rocks at it. One young bearded man walked up to the window on the outside and threw a large rock forcibly at Charlie's face on the other side of the glass. The glass splintered and he was showered with tiny pieces of glass but not seriously hurt.

Charlie inched his bus forward, slowly, a little at a time. Now the tear gas was sifting into the bus and he could barely keep his eyes open. He managed to get past Lincoln Park, down to North Avenue, where by this time, he could not see at all except for a quick glimpse.

Two police cars came blaring around the corner on their way to the riot. Charlie frantically flagged one down through the broken window. His bus stood straddled over the center divider in the street which was not where it should have been. When the officer approached Charlie he saw that his eyes were running tears. Charlie could not keep them open. His face was bright red and his hands shook. He told the officers he wanted to wait for the gas to dissipate and then get back to driving. The officers were not fooled by his bravado and took him to the hospital. His supervisor arrived soon after he did and eventually took him back to his bus. He told Charlie to dead-head into the depot without picking up passengers.

At the depot the Night Superintendent questioned him and after hearing his story told him he did not have to finish his run. By this time, however, Charlie was angry. "Those Communists are not going to keep me from working," He said. "I'll go get a cup of coffee across the street and then pull out for my last trip."

Once inside the restaurant Charlie realized he may have made a mistake. The dissident bus drivers were gathered there making the restaurant their headquarters and staging area for the mischief they were planning. The talk was loud. He heard quite a few threats. But none seemed to be aimed directly at him. So he calmly ordered a cup of coffee to go and left as quickly as he could.

Charlie walked slowly back to the depot. In the restaurant he had heard that about four hundred picketers were headed for this depot. He informed the Night Superintendent of what he had heard and then pulled his bus out before they arrived. It was strange how calm he felt right now. The things that had happened in the last couple of hours were unbelievable, like some bad dream. This could not possibly have happened. Not here in America, the free country where we were so united, so strong, the envy of the whole world. But it had happened. The Democratic National Convention was a mass of confusion and disturbance.

It was now 3:30 a.m. The rioting had been going on all night. Plate glass windows had been smashed in many businesses. Cars had been set on fire. There had been a massive struggle between demonstrators and police.

Charlie's last trip was uneventful. Usual early workers were going to work. They had no idea what had occurred during the night and he was in no mood to discuss it. Later there would be charges and counter charges, trials would be held, convictions obtained and sentences meted out. For now he wanted to get to the depot, park his bus and go home.

He drove the fifty-five miles to his home and entered his house. He was quite calm. He made a cup of tea and carried it to the front room, so as not to disturb his wife's sleep. Evidently she had heard him come in because she startled him as she entered the room. She took one look at him and cried, "Daddy. What's wrong?"

He was not aware that the tensions of the night showed that much. He said, "Oh, honey," and burst into tears. He told her the whole story from beginning to end while she sat close to him, holding his hand.

"Thank God you're okay," she said.

"Yes," said Charlie. "It could have been much worse for me but I'm home safe and sound now and I'm going to bed. I've got to work tomorrow, you know. All you have to do is mind your own business and nobody's going to bother you."

THE END

ANOTHER STORY
NEVER PUBLISHED

Another story that I wrote I titled *Nothing Ever Happens* where I had gone to work in the evening and Joe came up and said, "Hi, Chris."

"Hi Joe," I responded.

"How's things going?" he said.

"Oh, you know. You pick 'em up and you lay 'em down." This was an expression we had. You pick people up and you let them off and I said, "You pick 'em up and you lay 'em down, and nothing ever happens."

Joe said, "That's right. Same old stuff every night."

We both left. I worked on Clark Street and he worked on Touhy Avenue.

Here is the manuscript I sent in to magazines. Guideposts held it for a few months for possible publication, in 1975, and then decided it was too long and returned it to me.

NOTHING EVER HAPPENS
By
Charles M. Christensen

Charlie pulled into the parking lot of his employer, the Chicago Transit Authority on Foster Avenue near Kedzie. It was 8:30 p.m. He still had over half-an-hour before the start time for his bus run on Clark Street. He felt pretty good tonight. It was a pleasant night with a full moon. The temperature was around eighty degrees with a little breeze. He saw Joe pull in ahead of him, and after they had both parked their cars, they walked together toward the depot.

"Hi," said Joe, "How's things tonight, Preacher?

"Oh," said Charlie, "the same as always, Joe, you know. It's just getting started on the night's work. That is the hardest. After you're up there on the street it's always the same. You pick them up and you lay them off and nothing ever happens, same old thing, same people, with some exceptions here and there."

"Yeah," Joe answered, "I know. Sometimes, though, you find characters that bring a little spice to life out there."

"That's true," Charlie returned "but one thing always stands out in my mind about most folks. They're always trying to find a way of life that satisfies, something that will give them a lift, a bit of peace and security."

"Oh, oh," said Joe. "Here goes the preacher and the deacon again."

Charlie laughed. "Sorry Joe. You know me. I can't help telling others about the Lord. He IS real. Life is real and He is the creator of it. If you want real life you must go to the one who gave it in the first place."

Joe hesitated. "Yeah, I suppose you might be right. I don't know!"

As they entered the depot, other drivers greeted them. "Hey, Joe," "Hi, preacher," came from quite a number of the men gathered together, ready to take over their night shift of driving busses in the big city of Chicago. There was the usual joking, storytelling, experiences of the night before, and a few dirty jokes thrown in for good measure.

One driver came to Charlie as he did almost every night. "Hey preacher," he said. "I got a good joke to tell ya."

"Never mind," said Charlie. "I know your jokes, Tony. I'm not interested in your dirty jokes.

"Oh, this one's a clean one," said Tony, and he proceeded to tell his usual dirty joke. All the men knew what was going on. It had become a nightly pastime, trying to get the preacher going.

Charlie knew, too. He merely listened and made no comment until Tony used the Lord's name in vain. And then he had to warn him. "Tony, listen. The Bible says you had better not use the Lord's name in vain and warns of dire consequences if you do."

This brought the typical laughs and comments from the men. "Oh, well, Tony's going to hell anyway where his friends are." That kind of remark was normal. Charlie thought, forgive them father. They don't know any better, and he was silent as he smiled. He had a good rapport with the men. He was well-liked in the depot. Men had come to him in the past for counseling. He had led one driver to Christ one evening using the four spiritual laws put out by the Campus Crusade for Christ organization. Other drivers had been working nearby and could hear everything he told that man. This night Charlie finished copying his trip sheet for the night's work and turned to Joe. "Want a cup of coffee, Joe?"

"Okay," said Joe. "It'll help get the adrenaline going. I drink many cups every night just to stay awake."

After their coffee they walked out together to set up their busses. Charlie arranged his driver's seat to fit his physical needs for comfort, set the mirrors for good vision, both inside and outside, warmed the engine, and cleaned the windshield. It was imperative that his mirrors be kept clean and arranged properly because he used those mirrors constantly. They gave him a complete picture of the inside of the bus, both front and back, whether passengers were seated or boarding, or alighting from the bus.

Charlie took "defensive driving" lessons each year, in which every possible situation that might, potentially, cause an accident, was covered. For instance, in the fall classes he was warned that fallen leaves are as dangerous as ice on the streets. A bus can slide on crushed leaves as easily as on ice. He was ribbed a lot about being required to take these lessons after decades of driving, but he was justly proud, since the CTA had won award after award, for driving without accidents, or for fewer accidents compared to other companies.

Charlie, personally, had an excellent safety record. After more than thirty-five years of driving he had never caused an accident where anyone was seriously hurt. He thanked God every day for this record.

Charlie waved at Joe as he pulled his bus out of its parking place and past the other five-hundred-plus busses lined up in the yard. He drove out into Kedzie Avenue and began the twenty minutes of deadheading to his route for the night.

Clark Street ran from the Howard Street terminal at the northern city limits, south to the loop in the heart of the city. It is just over ten miles. He made four complete round trips each night. After the first two trips he had a fallback, or supper break, for thirty-two minutes and then he made two more trips. Each trip, including the layover, took approximately two hours, and with his pull-in and pull-out trips added, he received pay for a little over nine hours, five nights a week. He was off Saturday and Sunday nights.

It was good work, but more than that, for Charlie, it was a ministry. He had a chance to tell people about Jesus Christ, the Savior of the world. Some listened, some cursed, some just laughed, but that did not stop his testimony of the truth as he knew it from his own experience. He always had gospel tracts on his bus, wrapped in brightly colored cellophane paper, and rolled up like a cigar. Charlie believed that God used His word, as written in the Bible, to save people from their sins and he wanted to be faithful in planting the seed by telling them, if they would listen, about Jesus Christ.

Over the years some folks did receive Jesus Christ as their Savior. Most of the time Charlie's testimony was to people who rode with him only one time and he never knew if they responded to the gospel. But God did, and that was the important thing.

Charlie left Howard Street on his first trip at nine-thirty at night. His passengers were the usual workers who were coming from and going to work. He felt good. He had prayed for God's direction tonight, as he did each night. He was pleasant and people responded, generally, with a happy response.

At Diversey Parkway, about midway downtown, two teen-age boys got on the bus. One just walked in and the other stopped to put his fare in the fare box. "What about your buddy's fare?" Charlie asked.

"I ain't paying his fare," said the youth.

Charlie turned around in his seat. "Hey, son," he said to the other boy. "Do you want to come up and pay your fare now?"

The boy yelled at his partner that he thought he was going to pay the fare. His friend responded that he never did say he would, and so on. After a moment, with Charlie waiting patiently, the boy came forward to put his fare in the box.

"How much?" he asked.

"Oh, just the same as yesterday," Charlie answered. "It hasn't gone up this week at all."

The people near the front laughed. The boy glared at Charlie, paid his fare, cursed under his breath, and walked back into the bus, arguing with his buddy. Both had had a few drinks and were just letting off steam for recognition that they were grown up. This happened on a regular basis on the night shift. It is the "I have to prove myself" syndrome which was prevalent in those days. Some passengers got edgy during this time, never quite knowing what might develop. Charlie knew it was just part of the job.

After rounding the loop, and heading back north, Charlie picked up a boy who worked in the loop, and was a student at Moody Bible Institute. Their conversation was quite a blessing as they talked about the Lord and their ministries. It was always a joy to meet someone who knew the Lord. It was like meeting another member of the family.

Charlie's second trip into the loop was uneventful. It brought him back to Howard Street for his thirty-two minute fallback for lunch. He parked his bus in the terminal and went to the restaurant across Howard Street. He was well-known by the waitresses on duty at night and always had a time of kidding around with them and with the short-order cook.

Peggy, the elder waitress, was over sixty-five years of age but had the energy of a thirty- year-old. She was tough and efficient.

While Charlie was eating, a drunk came into the restaurant. His language was appalling, and uncomfortable for patrons to hear, so Peggy told him "get out and don't come back or I'll call the police."

"Call 'em," he said, "to ____ with 'em."

Peggy picked up the phone and dialed a number. The man took one good look at her, swore a couple of times, shook his fist, and walked out. Peggy put the phone down and continued serving her customers.

Charlie breathed a sigh of relief. He thought he was about to lose his supper time by having to go off to defend a disgruntled, unhappy person. He admired Peggy's courage. Any other waitress might take this kind of ill treatment from a bully, but she was not about to be intimidated.

Charlie finished his sandwich and went back to his bus. He pulled up to the gate, ready to leave in ten minutes. He was alone on the bus. It was 1:30 a.m. He had to leave at 1:40 a.m. on his third trip.

On his trip out of the loop he usually picked up a number of bartenders and maintenance people from the tall buildings, and some bank personnel, who worked the late shift. He had known some of these people for many years, such as Harry Schwartz. Harry had been working in a tavern for over thirty years, right in the toughest part of town, at Chicago and Clark Street. The back door of the tavern opened up into the parking lot of the police station. Many of his customers were policemen who frequented his tavern when they got off duty.

Harry got on the bus complaining and grumbling. He said he had nearly missed the bus because he could hardly get the last three policemen out of the tavern. He was uncompromising when it came to his closing time as dictated by the law. He was small, but tough, and solidly built, a Jewish man with a good sense of humor, about the same age as Charlie. They had a common bond. They both faced the same types of problems in their work and, therefore, could appreciate one another's difficulties. They had many stories to tell. The conversation between them was good, with others sometimes joining in, and the trip went fast for Charlie and for his passengers on their way home from work. It was a pressure relief time for many of them. Charlie was a good listener as well as a good storyteller. He was known as "the preacher" by many and they always expected some spiritual advice or a verse of Scripture along the way.

Charlie's last trip was his regular, ordinary, pick up of regulars going to work. He left at 3:40 a.m., picked up bakers, waitresses, a man in the youth division of the FBI, and two men who opened restaurants. One of them managed two restaurants. There was always a stranger along the way, going home after a night out on the town, but he seldom had problems at this time of the morning. Several of his passengers were construction workers who were building the new, tall, skyscrapers in the loop.

One time, a somewhat noisy drunk got on his bus saying he was not going to pay his fare that night. Charlie waited, with the door still open, for the man to put his fare in the box. He merely stood there, swaying slightly. When someone asked why the bus was standing still Charlie said, "Well, this man doesn't seem to want to pay his fare. I'm waiting until he decides what he wants to do. Pay, or get off." Two of the construction workers got up from their seats, came to the front and said, "Mister, pay your fare or get off. We're going to work and we don't want any nonsense from you."

The man who had sounded so rough and tough looked at them, dug down in his pocket and said, "Sure, sure, I was going to pay, just having some fun," but no one was laughing!

"Well, you can have some fun some other time," one of the workers said, and they all went back and sat down. Charlie thought I had that one figured right. He knew he had a backup crew on this trip. He called them shotgun riders. His plan was to try to play down violence whenever possible. The company seldom backed up employees in cases of violence, seeking to protect themselves from any kind of lawsuit for damages. Charlie understood and went along with this policy. It was all part of the job. He finished the trip back to Howard Street, delivering his passengers along the way, and headed for the depot. He felt good. He was not terribly tired. He knew driving home to Wonder

Lake, about fifty-five miles, would bring on the tiredness, and when he got home he would be ready for a good sleep.

He had left home at 6:15 the previous night and now, this morning, he drove to the gas pumps in the depot to turn in his cash box. He parked, and left this bus, and noticed Joe coming in from his run on Devon Avenue. He waited for Joe to park and they walked together to the depot.

"Hi, Preacher," said Joe. "How'd things go last night? It sure was a peaceful night on Devon Avenue. This weather, boy, it sure is beautiful, isn't it?"

"Yeah," said Charlie, "it sure is. I had a good night. It is uplifting to meet friends, old, and new, every day. You know, Joe, it is the same every night. You pick 'em up and you let 'em off. It's the same old story. Nothing ever happens but it's a good job, praise the Lord."

THE END

A YOUNG WOMAN
WHO NEEDED HELP

I became acquainted with many people during the fifteen years I worked the night busses on Clark Street and Broadway Street. Both runs ran down Clark Street from Diversey Avenue to Division Street.

There was a small, square, half block, park near the Newberry Library. It was called Bug House Square because, in the early nineteen-hundreds, men went there with wooden soap boxes, stood up on the box, and preached whatever they wanted to, whether it was against the government, or the gospel, or his own private war, whatever.

At the time my route ran past there, it was a park where men hung out. They walked, and sat around, and just loafed. Once in a while, a big, beautiful, car would drive up to the curb along the park and idle there. Someone from the park would approach the car, a conversation between that person and the driver would take place, and the person would get into the car which then drove off.

There was a young woman who stood on the corner of Belden Avenue and Clark Street, soliciting men for sex. I prayed for her. As I drove past where she stood one night, since she was close to the door, I said, "Hi. Good evening. How are you tonight?"

She nodded, and smiled, and said, "I'm fine. Thank you. How are you?"

After that, whenever I arrived at that corner, and she was there, I waved to her. She got on my bus one night and began a conversation. She said, "You know what I do for a living, don't you?"

"Yes, I think so," I said.

"I have a little daughter by a married man and I do this for a living," she said.

I asked her, "What are you going to tell her, about what you're doing, when she gets old enough to ask questions?"

"I'm never going to tell her," she replied.

I said, "Oh, that's foolishness. She will know what you're doing. It will never be kept from her. I know you make good money doing this, but you have to pay the syndicate a portion of your income in order to operate on that corner. Wouldn't it be better to have an ordinary job, making less money, but something that's honorable?"

She looked at me and said, "You know what? Do you believe this? I used to teach Sunday school."

I said, "Yeah, I can believe that. Perhaps you know you are on the wrong track. You need to change your ways and come to Jesus. He'll change you," and I told her how he had changed my life. She listened, and disembarked a few blocks later, and then each time I saw her, I waved and said, "I'll be praying for you."

She got on my bus again, maybe six months later, when I stopped at her corner. It was at least that much later. She said, "I got on to tell you I'm going to Pennsylvania for the cure. I'm really on drugs and I'm doing this to pay for my drugs. I'm going to Pennsylvania for the cure and I got on your bus to tell you I'm leaving, and to thank you for praying for me, and helping me." She paid her fare and got off at the next block.

I never saw her again, so I do not know what happened to her, but my prayers went with her. She could have been one of my daughters but for the grace of God, and so, I was concerned about her. Praise the Lord. He does the work.

JAMES

A man named James got on my bus many nights, at Howard Street, around 1:50 a.m., the time my run required me to be there. He stayed to almost closing time of the taverns, and then he walked over to board my bus. James talked with me about different things. He was usually pretty well inebriated, although not terribly drunk. He was able to walk even though he had been drinking all night. Occasionally, as I talked with James, I suggested perhaps, what he needed was Jesus, and I gave him many gospel tracts.

He got on one particular night and the first thing he said was, "You know, I went to a number of churches and talked to a number of pastors. I was trying to find out about God. But, no one ever told me what you've told me."

I said, "Well, that's strange. What churches did you go to?"

He named a number of different churches however; I do not think it is necessary to name them. He said, "I don't know what it is that you have, but I wish I had it."

I said, "What I have is salvation, full and free. It's a gift of God through Jesus Christ, His son. You need to recognize yourself as a sinner, and confess that to Jesus, and ask Him to come into your heart to be your savior, and that's what

He does. He changes your life." I quoted scriptures that verified what I told him.

James rode with me for, maybe, a year or two. We had a good relationship and talked about different things and became casual friends on the bus. Well, then for some time he was gone. I did not see him for six or eight weeks and I thought, I wonder what happened to James, where is James?

He got on my bus one morning on my last trip. On that trip I left the north end close to four o'clock in the morning and drove down to the loop, picking up early workers along the route. These were the people who opened up restaurants or bakeries or businesses and were on their way downtown before dawn. James was dressed as neat as he could be, he was cold sober, and I said, "James, hey, it's great to see you. Where are you going?"

He said, "I'm going to work and it's your entire fault!"

I said, "What do you mean, it's my fault?"

He said, "And I've got my kids with me."

I said, "Great. Are you taking them to Sunday school?"

"I sure am," he said. "I've invited Christ into my heart," and here was James completely renovated, completely turned around, just as I had been, and I praised the Lord with him.

James rode with me a couple of times and one night he boarded in the loop as I was coming toward the barn on my last trip. Now this was as we came north, when the sun was just breaking the horizon. It was a pale kind of light. A lady came up to the front of the bus to get off and she said, "This is the time of day that I enjoy walking along the lake front to watch the sun rise. It's so peaceful and wonderful."

I said, "Yes it is."

In the meantime, James had walked up to the front of the bus, too, and was standing behind her and I said, "The greatest peace that we can have, though, is peace with God through Jesus Christ, his son."

James tapped her on the shoulder and said, "Lady, you listen to this man. What he's telling you is the truth."

The lady laughed and said, "Okay. I'll listen."

So I gave her the gospel, told her how Christ had changed my life, and James' life, and that it is something she should consider if she did not know Christ as her Savior.

She said, "Thank you very much," and got off. She did not give us any comment one way or another, no testimony, no denial, she just went her way. I had given her some gospel tracts and away she went. So, the fact that James had witnessed along with me, was another blessing from God.

I had another experience on that two o'clock trip going back to the loop. When I arrived at Foster Avenue there was another drunk who got on my bus. I will call him Bill. He was a regular rider. He got on, paid his fare, and sat in the middle of the bus and he was blind drunk. I had learned previously that he worked for someone as a bartender, and I am sure he drank up half the profits this night because his speech was slurred, and he was absolutely drunk. He was not nasty or anything but he was drunk.

I began witnessing to him and telling him about the Lord and how God had changed my life. He was sitting in the middle of the bus and he kept saying disgusting words that begin with "b" and "s" and bull, and he kept repeating them every time I said anything to him.

People got on and off the bus during the trip, and when we got down to the loop at Van Buren Street, the only man still riding was Bill. He came up to the front of the bus.

This is what Bill often did. He rode down to Van Buren Street, where he got off, and walked to one of the large buildings down in the loop. Someone had taken these old, empty buildings, cleared off the floors, and set up partitions to enclose a four-foot by eight-foot space. They placed cots in each space, and rented them to men on the streets for a dollar, to a dollar-and-a-half a night. It was called a flop house. This night he had ridden with me to Van Buren and was leaving my bus to go to one of these flop houses for the night. As he was getting off I said, "Well, I gather from your comments that you don't believe in God."

"That's a lot of BS," he said.

"Oh!" I said, "Well, you have a perfect right not to believe in God. You know, God created us in his image, and he gave us a free will to use whether to worship him, or deny him, so you have a perfect right to do that. Even God can't stop you."

"It's a lot of BS," he repeated. I tried to hand him some tracts. "I don't want that religious junk. Keep 'em," he said.

I said, "Maybe we can be friends anyway," and I put out my hand to shake hands.

He said "Baloney," and nearly fell off the bus.

The next week, same time, same place, same trip, again, I was talking to somebody sitting up in the front of the bus near the driver's seat. The Lord had opened the door for me to talk about Jesus and to tell this someone about the tracts I carried, what they were, and what they said. Anyway, Bill came up to the front and I said, "I see you still don't believe in God."

"It's a lot of BS," he replied.

I said, "Listen, Bill, we can be friends, can't we? For goodness sakes there's no reason why we can't be friends," and I put my hand out.

"Uh," he said, "okay," and he shook hands with me.

Then I reached for some tracts and said, "Here, take these with you."

"No. I don't want them things."

I said, "Listen. You're going up to a flop house, you're going to lie on that bed, and you won't have anything to do." I said, "Read a couple of them. See what God has to say. Taste and see that the Lord is good, as the Bible encourages us to do."

"Uh," he said as I put them in his pocket.

I said, "Take them with you."

Well, again, seed was planted. Whether or not God brought him to salvation I will not know until I get to heaven.

THE COLLEGE MAN AND
THE PHILOSOPHY OF LIFE

On one of my earlier trips, as I was coming out of the loop, a pleasant man got on and we began talking. Apparently he was a college man and he talked about the philosophy of life. He explained his philosophy to me, and after he had been talking for a little while, he said, "What is your philosophy of life?"

I said, "My philosophy of life is centered in the person of Jesus Christ," and I preached the gospel. We went back and forth for a good twenty minutes or so, each giving our opinions and bringing forth our thoughts and sharing them together. At his stop he got up, shook hands with me, and got off the bus.

Another young man, similar to him in age bracket or so, came up to the front of the bus and said, "Did you major in psychology or something in college?"

I looked at him and said, "Son, I had a hard time getting through high school. I made it, but I had a rough time. The only way I got through college was to walk in the front door, down the hall, and out the back door. That was my entire college experience."

He laughed and said, "It sounds to me as though you are pretty well versed in life and its ways."

I said, "Well, for one thing, I deal with the public every day. I've been doing it for many, many years, and I have an open mind, and a heart. When Christ saved me at the age of thirty-nine, He gave me a renewed interest in people and their destinies." He was still listening so I went on. I said, "I believe in the Bible, I believe in the gospel, I believe in Jesus Christ and so I just share that with people as they get on my bus." He thanked me and got off at his stop. So that was another little experience that blessed my heart too. You see, when I talk on the bus, whoever is on the bus, hears me. I'm not quiet.

I know there are a few in my family, who love me very much, and who feel that I am a little bit over enthusiastic, sometimes, and that I blurt out things in places where, perhaps, I should keep my mouth shut. Some feel faith is a private matter, and although we should share it if people ask, we should not force our opinions on others. I entirely agree except when it comes to the gospel. I do not believe sharing the gospel is forcing it on anyone. God tells us to go into all the earth and preach the gospel and my bus is included in "all the world." If the door is open, one way or another, and I have a chance to preach it, I do. I do not apologize for that.

I know that I am a little facetious, and that God said we are not to be foolish, but I believe there is a certain amount of joy in the Lord's heart when I tell folks what he can do for me. I do not think he is too much against me, since he knows what I am made of, and saved me anyway. He knows how I operate. I know He will forgive me if I go a little bit overboard with witnessing once in a while. The gospel to me is Jesus Christ. Life is Jesus Christ. My family is, praise the Lord, under the heading of Jesus Christ, as head of the house, and I praise God for that.

123

OTHER MINISTRIES

We moved out to Wonder Lake, Illinois in 1970. We loved Wonder Lake. I had moved Grace out to that house on September 15, and later my mother, Anna Maria (Pedersen) Christensen and I came out on December 15 to stay.

We joined a Bible church in January of 1971 and I was active in the youth work. We did not have AWANA clubs in those days. We had a youth work of our own. We had a young pastor running some of that and I was active in it as much as I could be.

I taught Sunday school and eventually became Sunday School Superintendent for a number of years.

I was the Publicity Director for the church from 1977 to 1980. I learned how to write advertisements for the local newspapers from a book published by Moody Press. I loaned it to someone and it was never returned. That bothered me because I referred to it quite a bit.

If a singing group was going to minister at our church, I obtained a photograph of the group, and wrote an article about them. I included the dates of their appearance and said, "Pastor invites the public to come and hear," etc. I then took it down to the local newspaper in McHenry, Illinois before the ten o'clock deadline on Monday morning and handed it in. They printed it free of charge as a community service. Our McHenry newspaper was bought out by the Herald, which company owned newspapers in many small communities in our area. I have a huge collection of my writings over those three years.

Another activity we considered a ministry concerned Mrs. Wallach, who was a widow lady. Grace and I had been picking her up, and taking her to church, almost from the beginning of our ministry, until she moved to Chicago with her daughter. I think she was around 86 years old at that time. She used to save the Northwest Herald newspaper for me. When I picked her up on Wednesday night, she gave me the Monday through Wednesday editions and on Sunday she gave me the Thursday through Saturday copies. I took them home, and went through them day by day, and clipped out the advertisements I had written. This was a regular, accepted fact, that on Wednesday night for prayer meeting and for Sunday morning and evening services, we picked up Mrs. Wallach. It was a way of life, it was our social life, it was our desire, and it was our pleasure.

Mrs. Wallach was of German background and definitely old country and old fashioned. I believe she had quite a bit of money. She owned a little factory on Highway 31 on property that had all been purchased way, way back, when she owned a huge farm right there in the center of McHenry, Illinois. I am sure she had a fairly good income.

Mrs. Wallach now lives with her daughter. When we came home from vacation I wrote a note to her advising her that we had returned home and that we had a great time on our vacation, visiting our daughter. I told her we were concerned about her, and were thinking about, and praying for her. We learned that her daughter's husband had died, and that she was now quite busy with a new boyfriend.

Not being a Christian woman herself, she discouraged any contact between her mother, and the church, and her Christian friends.

Then we got news that a lady from Germany had become acquainted with Clara Wallach. She came from the same town in Germany that Clara came from, and was picking her up and taking her to church. So, we praise God for that answer to prayer and trust that Clara will continue to have fellowship with this lady. It is a pleasant thing to know that she is still being ministered to.

I was selected as an Elder of the church in Wonder Lake. At Mayfair Bible Church there were Trustees and Deacons. In Wonder Lake there were Trustees, Deacons, and Elders.

I was an Elder of the church for quite a number of years because, when the current Pastor came to us, it was decided that an Elder was elected for life. I was not in complete agreement with that, but I accepted it. The previous policy was that a man was elected to a three-year term. There were six Elders. Two would be elected each year. When your third year was up, if your name was submitted for Eldership again, you may be reelected.

In this past two years, three Elders have left the church. They were dissatisfied with some of the decisions of our new Pastor, and, while all three of them were critical of him, the last one did not separate his membership. He was still known as an Elder, but did not attend Elder meetings for a year. I wrote a letter to him, and called him up on the telephone, and now I am waiting to go with Pastor to visit him to determine what the problem is, although I think I know what it is.

It seems our Pastor married a young couple, who had been living together before they were saved. One of them had children. They had both come to Christ, and as Christians, they wanted to be married so Pastor performed the ceremony. This Elder was completely against this. He was dissatisfied and left the church.

WORKING WITH OUR PASTOR

Our Pastor is amazing. He does so much counseling that sometimes he gets overwhelmed with all he has to do. On Monday, his day off, he works for Tom Krause as a licensed paramedic. He goes out on calls on the ambulances. He does this for his own private satisfaction.

In his early years he was trying to determine if he should become a doctor or a minister, and the Lord called him into the ministry. He went to Toccoa Falls College, where he met his wife. After they were married he worked in Florida, then in Tennessee as an assistant pastor, in the big churches down there. I think there were five ministers in one church he served in. He also did building on the side.

He was with one congregation that got involved in a building program. He worked as much on the building program as he did pastoring and the deal became top heavy with building, and financially disastrous. There was a great deal of giving back and forth and he eventually left that ministry. That was one of the things he was questioned about when he came to us. You know, is he going to be the ruler or is he going to be the pastor? Is he going to be the man who shepherds the flock?

The first couple of years there was discussion among the Elders about some of the approaches our new Pastor took.

We met privately and decided to send a letter to him. Later on I concluded that sending that letter was the wrong thing to do. I confessed, to the Lord, that I was sorry I had done this wrong. I also telephoned the other Elders and told them I was sorry I had signed the letter. I went to Pastor and had it out with him in a kind, gentle, and loving way, and told him from now on I would back his ministry.

Pastor was a private person. When he came to us he had one little baby. Now he has two boys. One is five or six and the other three or four. He has opened up and blossomed out. He is still a private man and an exceptionally good organizer. Our church is moving in a fastidious way with all the committees and things. I am a man of rather lackadaisical approaches, letting things ride.

For instance, before Pastor came to us we had budgeted for a Christian school. We had it operating for three years, and then ran into debt. We had borrowed seven thousand dollars from our missions fund to keep our heads above water, so when Pastor arrived, we were in financial distress.

Since that time rules and regulations have been renewed and new ones begun. We now are required to send our mission money to New York immediately. There is no holding it back to pay something else with that money. We have a strict budget, set up by our budget committee, and we are now out of debt. We may be a month or two behind in payments here and there, or now and again, but Pastor is efficient in organizing and delegating responsibility. We have new members in the church, whose lives have been transformed by Jesus, and they have the ability to step in and conduct the business in a professional manner. I am not good at that. I am no longer on the Board. I desired to be off the Board.

As I said earlier, as an Elder I am what you might call a goffer, a troubleshooter. I fill in for our Pastor at various times, as the Lord leads, when he is completely swamped. I have an awareness of God's blessing when I am able to help him out. I know our church and he appreciate it.

I also go to AWANA club but only occasionally now. Last Monday night the AWANA leaders asked for help. So many kids were taking scripture memory tests that they needed extra help from people who were not actually leaders. These volunteers would listen to the children recite the verses they had learned, then sign off on their score sheets to show they had passed the test. Grace and I joined in and helped a number of children pass their tests. It was such a blessing to get back into working with the children. Grace and I love to be with the kids. They like us and we like them. I take time to talk to them. When they pass tests I do not just sign it and say okay. I ask them if they know what the verses mean, and if they say no, I explain it to them and try to help them understand what God is telling us in the Bible.

Grace and I have these various ministries. We like to invite people over to our house for a social time. We try to have six people, usually couples, but sometimes singles or a mix of couples and singles. We gather them together at our house, as our guests for dinner, with the expectation that they will become better acquainted with each other. We may serve a meal on a Saturday evening and then visit for a while. Grace and I enjoy doing things like this together. She loves to cook dinners, and serve them, and it is my job to try to keep her from getting too tired in these endeavors. We have a routine. We sit down to dinner with our guests and at the end of the meal I get up and start collecting dishes. I rinse, and stack them on the counter while the conversation is going on in the dining room. By the time I have finished, the others have moved into the living room, where I join them for an evening of fun and laughter.

We used to allow our guests to go out into the kitchen to help Grace wash the dishes, but by the time they were finished, it was time for our company to go home. So we now have the system I mentioned previously. Once our guests have left, Grace washes the dishes, stacks them in the drainer, and allows them to air dry. I dry certain silverware or silver urns with a towel and put left-over food away. I clear the table, and sweep the floor, little things like that. In about an hour to an hour-and-a-half we have completed the whole cleanup. In doing things this way we are able to join in on the conversation and the fun of getting to know people better. Also, our guests want to stay longer because we are not out in the kitchen, working away to clean things up, but are visiting with them.

Even when our daughter, Christine and her husband, Steve were here, she came out to the kitchen to wash the dishes. I was still rinsing. I said, "No way. You'll insult Momma. You go in the living room and visit and get to know these folks better. I'm coming in there right away."

We have invited leaders of the young people to bring a group here to sit around the fireplace and make popcorn, bake some cookies, and have soft drinks. Our home is open. We have not had a response to that yet, but I think we may, perhaps this winter some time.

Our church is looking for a youth director. We had set aside six-thousand dollars in the budget for a part-time youth minister. So we hired a man for a ten-month trial period. He had gone to Trinity College in Deerfield, Illinois. He agreed to minister with us for ten months and then we would decide if he was the man we were looking for. It was a two sided agreement. We would try him and he would try us. By the end of the trial period he and his wife had decided to become missionaries rather than to serve in youth work. We were pleased that he had this leading from the Lord, but then, we still did not have a youth director.

Nor did we have money to pay a full-time youth director. We needed a man like Clem to come in with his abilities and with a heart for kids. That would be something, although Clem now is in his music ministry, but he still deals with young people, I'm sure, within the church where he serves. It is a large church.

BOB THE HITCHHIKER

I occasionally pick up hitchhikers. I am told not to do that by my wife and daughter, and I understand why, but when I am alone, I do not mind doing it. I am under the Lord's hand and He will either protect me, or if something goes wrong, I am in His hands anyway. I no longer pick up hitchhikers when Grace is with me. I would like to but, she will not have it. No way.

There is a man, here in Wonder Lake, whose name is Bob. He has a great big belly on him. He is, perhaps, in his thirties. He was hurt as a high school football player, and apparently something happened in his head, and he is unable to work. He cannot hold a job. He is a little bit disreputable in appearance. He goes to either Woodstock or McHenry, and I think he hangs around the square, panhandling, although I do not know for sure what he does. He is not unintelligent.

One night, driving home from an Elder's meeting I was alone. It was ten o'clock at night and I came upon Bob in McHenry thumbing a ride. I stopped, and picked him up, and soon the conversation turned to talk about the Lord. He said he read his Bible, the New Testament, a lot, and he began asking me questions. So I began witnessing to Bob.

I drove him all the way to his home. He lives with his widowed mother in a house in the next subdivision over from where I live, and we sat for a couple of hours talking. He went into his house, and got his Bible, and came back out to sit in the car with me and talk some more. He asked questions and I explained to him how he needed to accept Christ as his Savior. I do not recollect that he did that.

Since that time, if I am going in to town and Bob is standing there in Wonder Lake, up on the corner, thumbing a ride, either to Woodstock or McHenry, and I am going the way he wants to go, I give him a ride, or at least take him up to Highway 120 where it is easier to get a ride.

Last Sunday Grace and I were on our way to church and there was Bob, standing on the corner, hitching a ride, and I had to wave to him and go on by. Earlier I had explained to him about Grace's uneasiness at picking up strangers. "My wife," I said, "has asked me to pass up hitchhikers when she's in the car. I respect her feelings and her fears. We have been advised not to pick up hitchhikers and although I know you, she does not."

He said, "That's all right, Charlie." One time, as I slowed down to pick him up, he shook his head when he realized Grace was with me. Apparently he understood her feelings also.

Occasionally I gave Bob a dollar or two and I would say, "Have a cup of coffee on me."

Grace and I were having a bite to eat in the Busy Bee one time, and I saw Bob sitting at the counter. When he was finished eating he came over to our booth and said, "Hello, Charlie."

I said, "Hello Ben. This is my wife, Grace." He talked with her for a few minutes and I invited him to sit down. "Have a cup of coffee," I said. So he sat down and ordered a cup of coffee and I encouraged him to order a Danish pastry, also. I would not have been surprised to learn that it was his second sweet roll, but I treated him, and then we took off and parted company.

Ben was not too clean (I should not sit in judgment of this) but I did not find him offensive. I do not know what his language was like away from me. He smoked, and when he got into my car, I asked him to put out his cigarette. Other than that, I did not know too much about Ben. I had a concern for him spiritually but I never knew where he stood with the Lord. Hopefully I will meet him again in Heaven one day.

PETERSON THE CHEAT AND A RUN-IN WITH A SUPERVISOR

You know, I wasn't always the 'goodie two-shoes' Christian man on my bus. When I worked on Kimble Avenue, in the rather early years of my driving, there were two high schools on my difficult, short route. The route went south on Kimball from Peterson Avenue to Milwaukee Avenue, merged into Milwaukee, and continued south to the elevated station at Logan Square. That was sixty-hundred north, down to twenty-eight hundred north, and around Logan Square.

I drove around the station to where passengers came down the steps from the "el" platform, and then drove back north. I worked on that line, driving behind a fellow named Peterson.

Peterson was, well, he was a cheat. He did not want to work. He wanted only to get paid. So he ran his schedule way ahead of time to avoid picking up passengers.

The busses were about five minutes apart at that time. If Peterson moved up to three minutes behind the bus in front of him, the time lapse between their busses would be only two minutes. Not many passengers arrived at the bus stops in that shorter time span. At the same time, he left three extra minutes for passengers to arrive for my bus, causing extra work for me. I was supposed to be five minutes behind him. If I ran on time, and he ran three minutes ahead of time, that caused an eight-minute headway between us. That meant I picked up half of his passengers, who had missed his bus because it was early, plus all of mine.

I thought I was as good a bus driver as he was and I did not have to take his cheating at my expense. I allowed it to go on for a bit, and then I thought, no, I am not going to take this. I am going to hold my headway. If he moves up three minutes, I will move up three minutes. I explained to the bus driver behind me, "Hank, Peterson runs up three minutes. I'm going to hold my headway, and I'm warning you, you'll have to do the same to survive this war we're having out here."

I followed Peterson and came in behind him at the "el" station off of Milwaukee Avenue. He was sitting there behind the station, hiding, and waiting until it was his time to pull out, and to drive down to where the elevated train station entrance was. That was where the Supervisor stayed. In other words, he came out from behind the station, with a halo around his head, supposedly running on time, and pulling up to the Supervisor, just like an angel. This upset me, so I pulled out right behind him, in front of the Supervisor, to make him aware something was wrong in the schedule.

The Supervisor came back to me and said, "What do you think you're doing? You ain't due here for another four minutes," and he chewed me out. I told him, "Ask Peterson where he was for the last four to six minutes." That did not make sense, because to the supervisor, Peterson was on time, and I was four minutes ahead of time, so he chewed me out. He did not get it that it was Peterson who was cheating.

That Supervisor rode me for a month. Every time I came down to his location, he had the watch on me. Every time I prepared to leave, he watched me like a hawk.

An incident occurred one time as I waited for my leaving time. In that particular place there was more than a foot-high curb. Peterson was standing on the curb at the front of my bus, watching me as usual. It was time for me to go. I admitted the passengers waiting for me, closed the doors, and started up, and he stepped down off the curb right in front of me! I was not expecting that, and frankly, I thought I was going to hit him. Praise the Lord, I did not. I stopped without hitting him. He came over to the door, and I opened it, and let him have it. I do not think, since then, that I have ever used the language I used on him at that time. I called him every name under the sun and blasted at him. I was furious. I was so upset I lost all my Christian testimony.

I drove up the street and dumped my passengers off the bus as fast as they wanted to get off. I did not pick anybody else up, if I could avoid it, and when I got to Foster I told the people waiting at the bus stop that they would have to take the bus behind me, because that was as far as I went. I drove across Foster Avenue into the depot. I did not go up to Peterson, but pulled right into the depot, and into the barn. The union steward came up to me and said, "Preacher, what's going on out there?" He said, "The boss is in the office, and his boss is in the office, and what's going on?"

I told him the whole story exactly as it had occurred. I told him the truth. He said, "They want to see you. We'll go in the office. Let me do the talking."

"Okay," I said.

North Park Transportation Building 1957

So we went into the office and Art Frank, the Supervisor I had the fight with, was there. The union steward said to my boss, "I want you to hear this man's side of the story. I want his side to be told here."

My boss's boss said, "I don't want to hear it." He said, "I don't care whether my supervisor was wrong or not, this man is suspended."

So I was suspended. That meant I had to go downtown to see the big boss. The union steward told me to write out what had happened, then go down to the union office, and give it to our union president. I wrote it all out. I even confessed, in the letter, that I had lost my testimony for the Lord, that I had asked God's forgiveness, and I asked Frank's forgiveness because of my filthy mouth. I wrote that

I still believed I was in the right. I went down and handed this letter to the president of my union, my representative, and he said, "The CTA has the power for discipline. You work under them and you'll have to take whatever discipline they hand out." I got no help from my union.

I was never a highly complementary man about our union anyway. I paid my dues but I was not always satisfied with their representation. Maybe you can see why. I grabbed my letter from this president of my union and said, "You just proved to me, that what I've always thought about this union is accurate. I'll take care of it myself," and I marched out of the office.

The next thing I did was to go to the CTA office. The head honcho there was a good man, a nice man, and he called me in to his office after a short wait. "Chris," he said, "What in the world is all this business? I've been looking at your record. You've got an excellent record. What is this?" and I explained everything to him. He said, "I don't know," he said, "they want me to have you put your badge on the table and for me to fire you."

I said, "Well," . . .

"They want you to quit."

I said, "I will not quit. If you want to fire me, you fire me, but I'm not quitting."

He said, "I don't know, I don't know what to say. The only thing I can think of is for you to leave here, and go straight back to Frank, wherever he is on duty. Sit down and have a talk with him. See if you can get this thing worked out with him. If he calls in, and tells me you two have worked it out between you, maybe we can allow you to keep your job."

I said, "I'll need a few minutes to think about this."

I had been off work for two-and-a-half days by now. I went out of the president's office, and into the corridor of the CTA building, and prayed. I telephoned Grace and explained the situation to her. I was thinking, we have two girls in high school, Rae Ann and Deanne, whom we needed to take into consideration. I explained to Grace, "I believe I'm right, I want to fight this all the way through to the end, but on the other hand, we've got the girls in high school. I do not want to lose my job. I don't know what to do." Grace said in her gracious manner, "You'll have to make your own decision." She always backed me up in the right things in our lives together.

So I sat down and prayed again. Finally, I went back into the president's office and told him, "I'll go out and see Frank."

I drove down to where Frank was working at a high school directing traffic and busses. I parked, and went over to him and said, "I'd like to talk to you."

"Come over to the squad car," he said.

I said to him, "I was told I had to come to you to get the matter between us settled. I apologize for cursing you. I am a Christian, and I should not use my Lord's name in vain, as I did. I've asked God to forgive me, and to wash me in the blood of Jesus, but I was so angry at you. I tried to explain to you what was happening, you would not listen, and then you stepped off in front of my bus, and I nearly hit you, and I lost my head."

He said, "When you cursed me I was ready to take you off the bus and really pound some lumps on you."

I said, "I wish you had. That would have, maybe, rid us of the animosity right then and there. I was ready for it. But I'm here now to see if we can settle the matter."

He said, "That's fine. Let's consider the matter settled. I'll call up the office immediately, you go back down there, and they'll reinstate you, and give you a pass to go back to work."

So that is what I did and I was reinstated. I had lost two-and-a-half days of wages. Frank did not lose anything; none of the bosses lost anything, only me.

However, I did learn a lesson. When I went back, the first day after this experience, I walked up to the clerk to get my run, and his greeting was, "Hello, fighter." Some of the men were behind me in all of this business. The boss himself, my immediate boss, called me into his office and told me, "Preacher, this went over my head. I had no way of controlling it. My boss took it upon himself to handle it. I had no say in what he wanted to do. Anyway, I'm glad it's settled."

And I said, "So am I. Praise the Lord."

I had a problem with a supervisor only one other time, when I was working on the streetcars, way back around 1940. His name was Logan. The only way he held his job is that he had an "in" downtown. He was somebody's somebody. He was an abrasive Irishman and a crude fellow.

We were approaching Lawrence Avenue one time, and my motorman had slowed down a bit before we got to Lawrence because we were a little ahead of time, maybe a minute or so. He cruised into Lawrence, and stopped as the light turned red, and Logan held him. When the light turned green Logan held him again. I got off the back end of the car and walked up to the front and said, "Hi. What's going on?"

Logan turned on me and cursed at me and said, "Who the h--- told you to come up here?" He used such foul language that I stared at him, and my mouth dropped open, and I said, "Are you talking to me, fella? You button up your mouth or I'm going to slap you so hard you'll land up on the sidewalk." There were, what we called, streetcar stops in the middle of the streets. They were raised cement areas and I told him I was going to slap him up onto that sidewalk. Logan had me suspended for a day. I had to report downtown to the CTA offices, I was chewed out, and I was sent back to work. My boss at the depot called me into his office and said, "Chris, this went over my head."

Now, this was before I was saved, and I was a rough, tough monkey in those days. I was not particularly afraid of anyone, but I was not a fighter either. I was a man of peace even as a non-Christian. I did, however, stand up for my rights. Those were the only two times that heavy disciplinary action took place in my workplace during the thirty-eight years I was employed by the CTA. Oh, once in a while I got chewed out for being ahead of time and maybe called into the office, but I was never suspended. I never lost a day's pay because of those minor infractions.

THE HORRIBLE BLIZZARD OF 1967

I remember the big snowstorm of 1967. Chicago was tied up with something like twenty plus inches of snow this particular night. I went to work on my bus Thursday night, and was on it until Saturday afternoon, before I was more or less rescued and relieved of my duties. Of course, I accumulated something like ninety-six hours of overtime at time-and-a-half in wages, which was not unpleasant.

The reason I worked so many hours is that there were cars parked along the street before the snow began. As the storm developed, and snow kept piling up, the snow plows came past them and threw plows-full of snow up on them, until they were buried. You could not see the buried cars. That night, if I was driving south with a load of passengers, and another bus came north; one of us would have to pull in between some of these cars to let the other bus past. We had to drive in the middle of the street. It was a terrible, terrible mess.

Some of the night busses were tied up in certain blocks and could not get loose. I had to go around Fullerton and Halsted, and down to Armitage, and back to Clark Street, picking up passengers, then down into the Loop. One other driver and I were the only two, out of about eight busses, that ran there, four on Clark Street and four on Broadway Street, that made it to the Loop.

Then, when I left Howard Street driving south on Clark Street, my last trip that night, I got one block away to where two busses were stranded, and stopped crosswise on Clark, blocking it off. There was no way I could go any farther south on Clark Street. I think I was the last moving bus on Clark and Broadway.

A block back, at Howard Street, there was an all-night restaurant and the man in charge there was smart. He had gone to the bakery early in the morning and ordered a lot of bakery goods. I went back to the restaurant, after being obstructed, and it was loaded with people. There were taxi drivers inside waiting to get hired. People came north on the elevated, if they could get north to Howard Street, the city limits, and then they hired cabs for transportation the rest of the way home.

Some young men came up with a good idea. They came to the end of the bus line with their vans and offered rides to people who needed to get home. They charged anywhere from three to five dollars to take them west on Howard Street. Some of those guys made good money during that day or two when the storm was at its fiercest.

The blizzard continued until late Friday morning. I think the accumulation was twenty-three inches, perhaps a little more. For at least two weeks thereafter the clean-up of the streets, and the removal of buried cars, occupied the city personnel. Some cars remained out on the street for three weeks before they were able to remove them. Workmen loaded up, and hauled off, huge truckloads of snow and ice, and dumped it in the Chicago River. Busses ran late for many days. It was a difficult time.

Later on, a man who was head waiter at one of the Big Diamond Jim's Restaurants downtown got on my bus often, and exclaimed to the whole load of passengers "This is the best bus driver the CTA has ever had. He's the only one that could get through the snowstorm." He ranted and raved about me and embarrassed me. He did this for two years! I did appreciate his gratefulness, though, and he made me feel good. He recognized my determination, that night, to give service.

It was awful for us bus drivers, and for the entire city, but because of that storm we now have 'snow routes.' A law was passed to limit parking on certain streets if snow accumulates to a certain depth. I forget now if it is two or three inches or whatever it is. That is the law that became known as the snow route law in Chicago. It is a good law because it keeps streets open during snowstorms. It gave officials the right to remove cars left on the street, perhaps inadvertently, with wreckers. The cars could legally be pulled off the street and taken to the impound lot where the owners had to pay to get them back. That fine gave folks the incentive to remove their cars from heavy traffic streets and to help us keep our busses moving. People still needed to get to work and they needed my bus.

1991 IN RETIREMENT

This is November 18, 1991. I am seventy-nine years old. It is a Monday night. I am alone in the living room again. Grace is reading. We have been living here for twenty-one years in this little house. It is a beautiful place to us with an all knotty pine living room, kitchen, and hallway. There are two bedrooms. We have converted what was an outside, cement-floored, porch into a cozy, enclosed, family room. I also bought the lot next door to us so that I have 125' of frontage on the road, and 150' going to the back.

I have had a garden for most of my years here; however, I eliminated it, permanently, this spring. I have no garden. I was thinking, seriously, that I might buy, maybe, four tomato plants next year, and just slap them into a little spot back there so we can have our own home-grown tomatoes.

God gave us this house. I know that. And, He gave us the car. He has blessed us down through the years. All of our family has been loving people to us. I just hope that – I know Grace has been a good Mom – I hope I have been a good Dad. I have heard a rumor, here and there, that maybe I had made a few mistakes along the way. I mean as a Dad, not in my own personal life, but whatever they were, I trust I got over them, or that I have been forgiven.

I have many fond memories where our girls and their husbands did things for us. For instance, one time Deanne and Bruce paid for a total week for all of us to spend it together down at the Lake of the Ozarks area, and we had a great time with them. That was the time I caught that huge Walleye. I also hooked another fish but it got away. We found it floating the next day, a great big fish with a long, flat snoot on it. It was called a Gar I think. I have a picture of me trying to hold it up while standing on the dock where we found it floating.

At other times we traveled to Rae Ann's and Jim's property on Table Rock Lake in Missouri, where we set up a camp a number of times, with our little trailer. That was always a pleasure. They took us all over the place. We took day trips south into Arkansas to visit some spots down there. We enjoyed Silver Dollar City two or three times. We went through that huge Marvel Cavern and then went into the Big Indian State Park and that was a great, great, time. I enjoyed that very much.

Thirty-nine years of my life was lived without knowing Jesus, but I always thought of myself as a good man. I did not chase women, I did not drink. However, I did have that terrible gambling addiction. My motives were always pure. If I won a lot of money, I could buy things for my kids, and my wife, and I rationalized it into a "good" thing, but of course, that was all phony. Still, I thought of myself as a reasonably good man. I was polite to people. I liked my job and went about it in a pleasant manner. I had been on the job fifteen years before I was saved, five of them driving busses.

God has given me an outgoing spirit, sometimes a bit overly outgoing. I am sure I have been criticized, both openly and quietly, by some who think I am too obnoxious, too but-in-ski. Whenever I meet a person, I open up by greeting them with, "Hi, how are you?" and if the Lord opens the door, or if anything comes up that will give me a chance to bring in the Gospel, I do it. I said before, that some people do not think this is a proper way to approach people, but how else will they find out about Jesus. If the only person they ever come into contact with, that knows Jesus is me, and if I do not tell them about him, how are they going to learn about God's gifts of redemption and eternal life? So I speak up. If I meet someone who is definitely against what I say I clam up. Nonetheless, as long as they are willing to listen, and as long as they have any questions, I try to give a testimony of what Christ has done for me, and of what he has done for them. I trust that they see his beauty as I put it before them.

WAS THERE A SERIAL KILLER ON MY BUS?

One night I came out of the loop with a busload of people, that is, seated people, nobody standing up, and I noticed a car staying behind me. When I pulled over to make a stop to pick up passengers, instead of going around me, that driver pulled up behind me, and stopped. As I continued north I thought this is strange, I wonder what this is all about. I thought of the possibility of a hold-up, or some type of crime that might be in process, so I kept watching. I figured, if anything truly suspicious arose, if I had a chance, I could grab the telephone and call a dispatcher.

I got about half way up my route on north Clark Street, and all of a sudden this car went zooming around me, swerved into my lane, and braked to a swift halt right in front of me. I had to brake too, or crash into him. Now there were flashing lights on the car. Two men got out and came to the door of the bus. I opened it and they boarded. This was an unmarked police car and these two men were detectives. One detective said, "Wait here for a minute. There's somebody we want to see." They walked toward the back of the bus, and faced up to a young man that was sitting there, and began asking him questions. They had him stand up. This looked serious to me.

This was the night that a fellow named Speck had killed six nurses. (Richard Speck, December 6, 1941 – December 5, 1991, mass murderer.) The police were out searching for him. My passenger apparently resembled the wanted man, or could have been him. At the time, I did not know what it was all about. I did not know what Speck looked like.

They brought my passenger up to the front door, and were about to take him off the bus, when the passenger spoke up and said, "Hey! I paid my fare. This isn't fair. I'll have to pay another fare because I'm not the guy you're looking for."

The policeman asked me, "Can you do anything about that?"

I said, "I can give him an emergency transfer that he can use whenever he's freed, and wants to get back on a bus. He can just get on and hand the transfer to the driver as his fare."

What drivers did, in this type of situation, was to take a regular paper transfer, punch six holes along the side of it, and form a capital letter E in it. That meant there was an emergency involving this passenger. Any driver would accept it as payment of the fare. It turned out that this man was not Richard Speck because Speck was captured later, and it was not my passenger. In fact, Speck is still in jail, trying to get out on parole, but he has never been able to do that.

PAY THE FARE OR PAY THE CONSEQUENCES

One night, on my last trip south into the loop, I picked up people going to work as usual. Some of them were truck drivers on their way to pick up their trucks to haul gravel, sand, and road work equipment. I had, maybe, a medium seated load of passengers, mostly men, riding with me that trip. I came down to Foster Avenue, stopped at the bus stop, and opened the door, and a drunk got on. He began raising a fuss. He said, "I'm going to ride with you, and I ain't got any money, and I ain't gonna pay ya."

I said, "If you don't pay, you don't ride, you'll have to get off." I had shut the door and stepped on the gas. He argued and debated with me about not paying. I had driven across Foster Avenue, heading south on Clark Street, but then I pulled over to the curb, parked, and just sat there.

Some of these tough guys on the bus said, "Hey, bus driver, what're we sittin' here for?"

You know, you learn to use the tools you have. I said, "Well, fellas, I'm sorry, but we've got this guy on here. It sounds like he's been having a good time tonight. He doesn't want to come up with the bus fare, and I am not going to move 'til he pays the fare."

As I thought might happen, three of these tough looking men got up out of their seats. They were not together, either. They came up to where the drunk had sat down and said, "What's the story, here, bub?"

The drunk got up and said, "Ha, ha, ha, I was just tryin' to have a little fun."

"Yeah, well have a little fun some other time. Put your fare in the box!" one of the men ordered.

So the drunk stumbled up to the front, put his money in the fare box, then sat down and did not say another word. About a mile later he got off. But, you see, I had my shotgun riders riding with me again that morning, and all I had to do was pull over, and let them take care of business for me.

That is also what I did that time with a busload of students from Lane Technical High School. When I went into the turn-around at Roscoe Street I took on a busload of passengers, pulled out into the street, and had not gone a block, when I heard a crashing sound in the rear. In my mirrors I could see where a window had been smashed, and then I heard another window smashed in the back. I looked again, and saw a third window was cracked, in the rear. The students were all rough housing back there. I pulled over to the curb and parked. I did not say a word to anybody. The kids were yelling, and screaming, and wrestling, and pushing each other, and I just sat there. I must have sat there two, three, or maybe four minutes, when all of a sudden they noticed the bus was not moving down the street. One of the students hollered out, "Hey, bus driver. What are we sitting here for? Why ain't we moving, what's wrong?"

"Oh," I said, "nothing kids, I'm just waiting for the police."

"What?" They sounded surprised.

I said, "I'm waiting for the police, I called the police." I said, "You guys think you can get on my bus, and break up seats, and crack windows, and get away with it. Well, you can't. I'm going to have you all hauled into the police station."

Then the pleas began. "Oh, Mr. bus driver, please don't. Get going before the police get here." They were a pitiful bunch.

I said, "No way. I have to report those broken windows to my supervisors. They're going to ask me why I didn't call the police." I said, "I've called 'em and I'm going to . . ."

There was more pleading and begging. "Oh, please, bus driver. Go before they get here. We'll be real quiet. We won't make any more noise, we won't do anything wrong, we'll quit fighting. Please go."

I took off. I had not called the police. I just wanted to get them settled down. But, when I got in to the barn, of course, I had to make out a report of broken and cracked windows which had been done by the kids from Lane Technical High School. I reported that I could not catch them, and actually, I had not seen who damaged the windows.

Many times, when things of this nature arose, I tried to gauge proper procedure, and most of the time I tried to avoid direct confrontation, or fights, because it did not pay to get into one. In those days, there was a lot of rough stuff where I drove. Some men carried knives. There was not a great deal of shooting back then. There were no neighborhood punk gangs, as we have in this day and age. There were gangs but they were men. They were businessmen, and they fought among themselves, mostly. Now-a-days, if you say a wrong word, or tip your hat the wrong way, you are liable to get shot, and it still does not pay to fight over anything.

THE BARTENDER'S KINDNESS

One of the nicest things that happened in my fifteen years on the night busses concerned a Jewish man, who was a bartender, in a tavern on Clark Street, just south of Chicago Avenue. It was directly behind the Chicago Avenue police station. His name was Harry Schwarz and he seemed quite intelligent, and he was friendly. He said he never drank anything at the bar. He was in the business as long as I worked for the CTA, thirty-eight years.

Harry used to close up the bar as I was driving south on Clark at around 2:00 a.m. when I came to Chicago Avenue. As I crossed Chicago Avenue, I would look west along that street into the tavern to see if Harry was closing up, and if so, I might wait a few minutes to pick him up. If not, if he waved, then I would go downtown to Harrison Street and come back north on Dearborn, one half-block east of the tavern. When I got back to Chicago Avenue I would turn and look down Chicago, and most of the time, Harry would be there waiting for me.

There were a lot of policemen who frequented Harry's bar. Sometimes Harry had to get rough with them at closing time because bars were required by law to close at 2:00 a.m. If he did not close, the policemen are supposed to arrest people, or at least come in and close him up, but who was going to arrest the policemen?

Harry used to tell them, "Why don't you guys go home to your wives? Get out of here," he would tell them, as he pushed them out the door, and made them leave.

Harry and I developed a friendship. He usually rode all the way to the end of the line, Howard Street, and then, if he could find a cab, he would take a cab from there. If there were no cab, he rode back to Touhy Avenue with me, to where he could catch the last Touhy Avenue bus going west. Busses did not run all night on Touhy.

Harry and I had many, many conversations. He knew my testimony. I had witnessed to him and talked about the Lord Jesus Christ. Part of Harry's family lived in Phoenix, Arizona. They were Orthodox Jews. He told me about the Orthodox approach to religion. Harry was not religious himself, but every Christmas he gave me a gift. He always gave me a bottle of whiskey. I did not want to refuse it.

When we were living on Irving Park Road, the doctor prescribed that my Dad should have one ounce of some kind of brandy every night before he went to bed. That was supposed to be good for him. So I asked Harry if I could buy a bottle of cherry brandy from him. He got on my bus one night and gave me a bottle of brandy. He refused to let me pay for it, and I said, "Harry, if you don't let me pay you for it, I'll be ashamed to ask for it the next time I need another one."

He said, "Never mind, just ask," so he gave me cherry brandy for Dad.

In those days, Grace made homemade date-and-nut bread in those #2-size tin cans that vegetables came in. I brought Harry two of those loaves of nut bread one time, as a gift, and said this was for him and his wife. He bragged that up for the next year. He said his wife truly loved that bread, and he was appreciative.

Every year Harry sent me a Christian Christmas card with a five dollar check in it, until three or four years ago, when the cards no longer arrived, although I believe Harry is still alive.

One day, I had to go into Chicago for something, and I took the time to go way up on Touhy Avenue, where he worked part-time, in a laundry, and I saw him. I talked with him for a few minutes, but of course, he was busy working there, and he could not just talk forever with me. He had already had lunch so he could not go with me somewhere to eat. We said goodbye. I have not heard from him for a long time and we stopped corresponding. Harry Schwarz, a good man. I always thought of him as a good friend, and we had a lot of good times together on that drive north. It was always a forty-five minute drive from where he got on in the loop, and it was a good time of companionship. I always had company on the bus, which made it nice. It kept me awake. So Harry Schwarz, a good friend.

THE MAN WHO COULD NOT SLEEP

There was one other incident that went on for a few years. A man, who limped, boarded my bus and paid his fare. His name was John Rodgers. Many nights he rode up to the end of the line, and when I turned around to go south again, he paid another fare. He told me he could not lie down to sleep because of a steel part in his leg, and so he slept, sitting up, on my bus. He rode with me most of the night. He worked for a photo place that developed negatives, down in the loop. After a couple of years of riding with me he lost his job. He was down and out on the street with no place to go.

John was neat most of the time. He had little money and so, if he got on and paid a fare, I let him ride all night on that one fare. Occasionally, when I arrived at the end of the line for my fallback, I said, "Come on John, let's go over and get a sandwich." It was my treat.

John rode with me two or three times a week because I was the driver who let him ride all night. In fact, when I returned from vacation one time, my replacement driver said, "John Rodgers is waiting for you. He wanted to ride all night with me but I did not let him." So when I got back on the street, John Rodgers rode with me, and that went on for a couple of years.

John was absent along my route for six months or so. Then, I came down into the loop one night, and stopped to pick up passengers at Madison Street and Dearborn Street, and John was there waiting for me. He boarded, and I nearly did not recognize him. I had never seen a more disreputable looking, more down-and-out, miserable, piece of human flesh in all my life. John was obviously in terrible pain. He gave me a transfer, which I accepted without even looking to see if it was good or not. I just took it. He limped down the aisle, all the way to the rear of the bus, and sat down. I continued driving the route, and when we arrived at the end of the line at Howard Street, he stayed on, and rode into the turn-around. I turned in my seat and said, "John. What in the world has happened to you?"

He struggled up to the front and sat on the long seat across the aisle from my driver's seat and said, "I don't know what to do. Charlie, I'm sick." He pulled up his pant leg to show me the sores all over his leg. His leg was a horrible looking sight. It looked moldy to me. It was a rotten looking leg. He said, "I went to Cook County Hospital and they would not do anything for me. I don't know what to do."

I said, "John, I'm going to give you a transfer. Ride with me to Madison Street, and then catch a bus east to Morgan Street, where you'll get off. Then walk a block south on Morgan Street to the Christian Industrial League. It's a mission," I said. "They will take you in. You're going to ask for this particular man whose name I put on the note." I handed him the note I had written to the head man at the mission.

I had ministered to folks at the Christian Industrial League, with friends from Mayfair Bible Church, a number of times. I had led singing, given testimonies, and had witnessed to people, hoping to lead them to Christ.

159

Anyway, I gave this note to John, and encouraged him to go to the mission right away. I said, "You may be a little early but they open at six this morning. Ask for this man, and give him this letter, personally." I let him off at Madison Street. John disappeared again.

Christian Industrial League has a huge warehouse full of clothes, shoes, overcoats, and accessories for people in need. When someone comes in to the mission, the workers treat him as they would any other person who is doing just fine, with one condition. The needy person must remove all of his clothes, and then take a hot shower to be rid of lice or other pests before they will give him clean clothes, a room, a bed and food. They keep the mission sanitary by doing this.

To my surprise, one night, six or eight weeks later, I drove into the loop on my run, and there was John Rodgers, waiting at the bus stop, dressed in a suit and tie, with nice shoes, and he looked quite presentable. He told me he had gone to the mission, and given the note to the man I had written it to. My Christian friend had read the note, and talked to John, himself. John showed him his infected leg, and he immediately took John to the Cook County Hospital in a taxicab, and they treated him.

John was not a drinker or a drug user. He was straight, and although he was not open to the gospel, he did listen to me. He never showed signs of being willing to accept Christ as his savior. Now here was John, ready to go back to work.

I spoke to him about applying for a green card. A green card in Chicago would give a needy person a place to stay. I think it was a room, at Chicago Avenue and Dearborn Street, in an old YMCA. He was there for quite a while. The City gave him a room, and an amount of money for food, and he sometimes rode with me at night. After that I do not know what happened with John.

Just before I retired – I had only a night or two left to work – I came into the barn and one of the other drivers said to me, "Hey, Preacher, John Rodgers was looking for you."

I said, "I may not get to see him again. I'll be gone in a night or two. I've retired."

He said, "John said something about wanting to pay you back the money he owes you." I had loaned John thirty-five dollars when he needed something.

"Praise the Lord," I said. "If he gets on my bus, great," but I did not see John again. I often pray for him, and I wonder how he made out in life, and what happened to him.

GMC Bus 1178 NB on Lake Shore Dr. 1973

161

THE MAN WHO TRIED MY PATIENCE

Another man that took a lot of my time, off and on for eleven years or so, was Bob Kennedy. I was out on one of our visitation ministries with Mayfair Bible Church. A group of us went in twosomes, door to door, ringing bells, and asking folks if they had a Bible. If they did not, we asked if they would like to have one. We gave out quite a few Bibles this way.

Mrs. Ewing and I were teamed up together one night, and who answers the door? Bob Kennedy and he said, "No, we don't have a Bible. I'd like one. Come on in." We went in and sat at the kitchen table talking with Bob. He had been drinking, there was no question about that, and while we were there, his older brother, Jim, came into the room. Actually, Jim came in to throw Bob out of the house. We did not know that at that moment. Bob introduced us to Jim and explained to him why we were there.

After talking for a few minutes, I convinced Bob to come over to the church with us to talk with our pastor. We all explained the plan of salvation to him from the Bible, and Bob eventually made a profession of faith in Christ. However, Bob was an alcoholic.

As time went on, I would get a call from his mother at night saying, "Charlie, do you have any idea where Bob could be?"

I would say, "No."

She would say, "He isn't home."

"I'll go see," and I would chase after Bob, and try to find him in a tavern, and get him back to his house. One time, he wrote checks on his mother's savings account, and wound up in Statesville Correctional Facility for two years. I visited him down there in prison. When he was released, I picked him up, and brought him back home.

Bob was at our house one Christmas, and the next day we went in to talk to Pastor again. He confessed his sin in prayer to God and asked Christ to come into his heart. He wanted to change his life. But Bob Kennedy did not change his life.

He took a room over on Irving Park Road down near the six corners. I gave him ten dollars to help out. He told me a couple of years later, the last time I saw him, that he had used the ten dollars to buy a bottle because he had a woman up in the room. Bob was not faithful to his commitment to the Lord, and I felt sorry for him.

I was in the church alone, working on my duties as Sunday School Superintendent, when Bob entered the church. He came in and down the steps to the Sunday school office. He was drunk. He was feeling terrible. He wanted to know if I could give him some money. He said he HAD to have a drink. He was having tremors, or whatever it is called, coming out from a drunk, and he wanted a drink. I said, "I'm not going to buy whiskey for you, Bob." He went in one of the Sunday school rooms and proceeded to throw up all over the floor. I had to clean it all up.

I had sent him down to the Christian Industrial League previous to this. They had taken him in, and given him a room, and he had actually been driving a truck, picking up things they needed from the warehouse. He must have been down there a couple of months. Then they caught him with a bottle in his room one night and they threw him out.

A month later he was living in the park up at Foster Avenue, sleeping in the park. He came to me this day after having been out on a hoot. He was coming off this drunk and he needed a shot. He had to have a shot. He was going into DTs (delirium tremens). I said, "Bob, you have got to go back to Industrial League. Confess what you did was wrong and try again to get back in there."

He said, "I gotta have a drink."

I gave him a couple of dollars, and then he leaned over the fountain to get a drink of water, and some papers and bills fell out of his shirt pocket. He had three or four dollars besides the two I had given him, so I was rather disgusted with him.

I drove Bob up to Lawrence Avenue near Elston Avenue, hoping to get him on a bus down to the Industrial League. He said, "Charlie, I must have a drink."

I said, "I'll take you in to a tavern and I'll buy one drink for you. Will you walk out after that?"

He said, "Yes."

We went in to a tavern, and I bought him a shot of whiskey, then ushered him outside again and walked him to Lawrence Avenue, where I put him on a bus. I said, "You go down to Broadway Avenue or Clark Street, to the Industrial League, to see if you can get back in there." That was the last I ever saw of Bob. I do not know what ever became of him. I have often wondered.

Pastor Charles Bartels said, "I don't know how you could have had all that patience with Bob. You've been following this guy, off and on, for eleven years. I would have given up a long time ago."

I said, "Pastor, God never gave up on me, so I can't give up on Bob." God can change his life, and will change his life, if Bob ever truly repents.

The first time I brought Bob home drunk with me, Grace took our girls into their bedroom, and not only closed the door, but pulled the dresser up in front of it. She instructed them on how to go out the bedroom window. Grace would lift the girls out through the window, and then she would climb out, and that was the way they would escape.

In the meantime, I went to bed in our bedroom, and Bob Kennedy went to sleep in Grace's bed, and I never gave it a thought. I had a good night's sleep. But Grace thought it was foolishness and she was scared. I recognize that now. It WAS foolishness; however I never gave thought to those things. I was doing the Lord's work. I was trying to help a person. I was reaching out with the love of God, and I never gave it proper thought. I should have given it more serious consideration. In fact, there came a time when I apologized to Grace, and promised I would not bring home any more drunks from off my bus.

One time, though, I did bring a young man home once again. He was homeless but not a drunk. I had told him I could not take anybody home with me, and he said that was all right, he understood. I did not know what to do, because it was frigidly cold, and he had nowhere to go. I reconsidered, and took him to our house, and down into the basement and Grace heard us. I went upstairs to explain to her that I had a young man home with me and she said,

"I know," and I said, "I don't know what to say, honey, I could not leave him outdoors. Its ten degrees below zero out there." This was in March. Wonderful woman that she is she said, "Bring him upstairs." I brought him up to the kitchen and Grace cooked bacon and eggs for us. Then he had a bath, which is what he wanted in the first place. After that nice hot bath, he went to sleep down in the basement where we had an extra bed. The next morning he went to church with us.

CURRENT DAYS

Grace and I have reasonably good health, considering our ages. The doctor said my health is average to poor because of the heart business. I do get a little bit upset with my inability to function physically. I cannot do much without losing my breath quickly. I have to sit down. God has always blessed us.

I sat last night, alone here, and I went through pictures that we have organized in albums from down through the years. Some of the pictures brought back memories. For instance, when Rae Ann and Deanne were small, Grace made outfits for them. As I look back, I think it was because she did not have enough money to buy clothes in those days. Maybe that was it, but, she always sewed beautiful little outfits. I have a picture on the wall, taken in the park, with Deanne, sitting on my knee, in one of those outfits. People always complimented Grace on her beautiful, intricate needlework. She was truly talented, and creative, and meticulous in her work.

I remember we used to go out to Wilmette, where that Baha'i Temple is located, with my Dad and Mom. Dad and I went and fished out on the pier, or I played with my daughters. I loved them, although my thoughts, in those days, before my salvation, were that I worked to earn a living, and Grace raised the kids. My daughters were fifteen and thirteen before I ever came to Christ and began to think differently. I guess they got by, and they seem to have turned out pretty good. At least I think they did.

The older I get, the more I realize that everything is held in the hands of God, and through Jesus Christ, his son. I try not to inflame people anymore. I try not to press people about spiritual things, although, maybe, I miss that goal once in a while, especially with my kids. I love them dearly, and I push them a little here, and a little there, because I believe our lives are centered in eternity, not in the present world. We live in the present world but we are not of the present world. God blesses us in the present world with our work, our money, our income. What we do with it – that is another question. That is enough preaching. I have said my piece, amen, praise the Lord.

THE LAST STORY

Now I am going to tell you the story about the last two weeks before I retired. This might be thought of as the end of my ministry as "the preacher" on my bus.

I worked Monday night through Friday night, five days a week, on a run that paid nine-and-six-tenths hours which gave me forty-eight hours of pay a week. Then I was off Saturday and Sunday.

I had been living in Wonder Lake for the last three-and-a-half years. I drove the fifty-five miles to the barn in the city every night, and as I was driving that Monday, I prayed that the Lord would use me as a testimony. I had ten days to go before I retired, and I prayed and said, "Lord, cleanse me, make me a fit vessel for your use tonight. If it pleases you, Lord, this week, bring somebody to my bus each and every night, someone you wish to speak to through me. Give me the Scripture, and the leading of your Spirit, to speak to them of yourself, and your wondrous salvation, and the grace that you extend to them."

It was amazing. Every night the following week, those five nights, somewhere along my bus route, somebody boarded the bus, and I began a conversation as I usually did, and I saw openness to the gospel like never before. I talked about Jesus, and gave out tracts, and talked to people. When we arrived at their stop we said good-bye and they left the bus. Every night! At least one person got on with this openness. Sometimes, perhaps, I spoke to more people, but every single night, someone was attentive to the things I had to say about the Lord, and about His salvation.

The following week on Monday, with only five nights to go before I lost my pulpit, so to speak, my bus driver's seat, my ministry, my vineyard, which bothered me a little, I prayed that the Lord would open other vistas for me in the church ministry. There were openings over there at the church. But, on this Monday night, again, I prayed for cleansing. I prayed, "Lord, make me a vessel of honor tonight." And then I prayed this prayer. "Lord, I know your Word does not return unto you void, but that it shall accomplish that for which you sent it. I witness often, I pass out tracts, I plant the seed, and people get off and then I never see them again. And so, I do not see results very often. I did with John, with Patty, and others down through the years, and one driver I led to you in the depot while we were writing up our runs, various times like that. But, it isn't often that I see this, and if I've found grace in your sight, will you show me tonight, somewhere along the route, a bit of evidence of your salvation?" And, I went to work.

At two-forty in the morning, I came out of the loop on my last Monday night, and came up to North Avenue on Clark Street, where two young people boarded the bus. A young woman with a blank drawing board, about three or four feet square under her arm, and a young, handsome man with long hair down to his shoulders. They were not together. They each handed me a transfer off the North Avenue bus. She sat directly across from me, on the long seat, and he went to the middle of the bus. Well, Smart Alec

Charles, you know him, he is always opening his big mouth and I looked at her and I said, "Did you get on my bus to paint my portrait?"

"No," she said, "not really," and she smiled.

"Oh. Okay," I said. "Did you know that I'm an artist?" That caught her attention a little bit.

She said, "You are?"

I said, "Yes. I like to paint the portrait of the Lord Jesus Christ on the hearts and minds of people so that they may see his beauty."

"Oh," she said. "Well." She stood up. "I'm sorry," she said, "but I'm not into religion."

She rode only four blocks from North Avenue to Armitage Avenue and when she said I'm sorry, I said, "Well, I am too, to hear that. But I wonder if you will allow me a pleasure?"

She said, "What's that?"

I said, "I would like to give you this little white booklet. It's a portion of Scripture, they're called Little Bibles, and they have verses from the Bible, and I thought perhaps you would accept one of these as a gift. It's no big deal, but I thought I would like to give you one, if you're willing to accept it."

She looked at it and said, "Okay," and reached out and took it, and got off the bus. I prayed, "Lord, please bring fruit," and I went on my way.

I delivered my passengers as they got off the bus, and when I was about six or eight blocks from the end of the line, this young man with the long hair, the last one on my bus, came up to the front, and stuck his finger in my face, and said, "You're the God man, aren't you?"

I looked at him with astonishment and said, "Well, son, I don't know exactly what you mean by that expression, but I am a Christian and I preach Jesus."

He said, "That's what I mean. You know that little white Bible you gave that girl that got off at Armitage?"

I said, "Yes."

He said, "You gave me one of those a year ago and it's still on my dresser."

I said, "Praise the Lord. That's great. Tell me. Did you ever become acquainted with the author of that little Bible?"

"Yes," he said. "I've invited Jesus into my heart to be my Savior. He changed my life and I am now trying to tell others about him. Do you have any more of those little Bibles that you could give me? I'd like to give one to every member of my band."

"Well! Wow! There was the answer to my prayer, and I told him, "You are an answer to prayer tonight. You don't realize that, but you are," and I emptied my pockets of everything I had in the way of the Scriptural sense, and handed them over to him, and I said, "Pass them out. Tell others about Jesus," and he thanked me, shook hands with me, and got off.

Well, I do not suppose people will believe this, but when I got into the barn, and then into my car to drive the fifty-five miles home, the car's wheels were at least four feet off the ground. And I was praising God the whole distance. I'm still praising Him today because God spoke to me through that experience. He said, "Charlie, why do you always get all upset about the wrong things. You just plant the seed. I'll take care of the increase. Just trust me." And I said, "Yes, Lord. I hear you."

AFTERWORD

Charlie and Grace, my Mom and Dad, came to live with me and my husband in September of 2000. He was 88 years old and she was 86. He had been caring for Mom, who had Alzheimer's disease, for at least five years before it became impossible for him to do it on his own. She died in May of 2012 at the age of 98 years.

One morning, about eight weeks after they came to us, Dad was trying to figure out his check book balance, but he said he could not get the figures to balance. He got up from where he had been sitting at the dining room table, and stumbled forward in a couple of steps, until Jim and I caught him, and steered him over to the couch. He passed out. We called 911. The paramedics were there in no time, and as they were leaning over Dad, he came to, and was quite agitated. He complained that he thought he was on his way to heaven and here he was, right back here on earth! He was disappointed.

He was in the hospital for twelve days and in and out of consciousness. Mom did not know who he was and thought he was her grandfather. She would not stay at the hospital for more than an hour. Then Jim or I would have to take her home, and one of us would have to stay with Dad. Mom was not upset. I think she did not actually know what was happening.

I learned that the doctor considered Dad to be terminal, and told him in one of his wakeful times, that I thought he really was going to be with Jesus. He smiled. I told him not to worry about Mom, that we, the family, would take care of her, and he passed out again.

He woke one other time as I was standing at the foot of his bed. He roused a bit, looked me straight in the eyes and said, "Be brave," and passed out again. He did not regain consciousness, and died two days later in November of 2000 at the age of 89-3/4. I often wonder if, after he got to Heaven, a couple of people he had witnessed to during his many years of bus ministry came running up to him shouting, "Hey, Preacher, where have you been? We've been waiting for you."

CPSIA information can be obtained at www.ICGtesting.com
Printed in the USA
LVOW08s0553080714

393233LV00002B/3/P